2-99
(21)

forty-nine days

A companion to accompany
the forty-nine days following a loved one's passing.
For the one left behind
and the one who has moved on.

By

Mynavati

forty-nine days

Copyright Mynavati © August 2007

Cover Design & Layout, Craig McQueenie - craig@giantdesign.co.uk

First published in India in 2008 by:

The School of Ancient Wisdom
Kannamangla Palya,
Post: Kannamangla,
I.V.C. Road, Devanahalli 562110,
Karnataka, India.

Printed and bound in India by

Sri Ayyappa Printers
Bangalore - 560 027

ISBN 978-81-906575-0-1

Dedication

This work is dedicated to
all who have been bereaved,
to all who are suffering
the loss of a loved one and
to all who will be bereaved.

About the Author

Mynavati, meaning she who dispels delusion, is a spiritual counsellor, dreamworker, retreat leader, healer and author.

She has worked extensively with those suffering loss and has helped people who have been bereaved as well as having had life-changing personal encounters with loss, death and near death experiences herself.

Born in Edinburgh Scotland, she has travelled to the far corners of the world in search of her True Self. Mynavati was brought up as a Christian but has spent many years studying and living with holy men and women, in particular with Tibetan Buddhist, Advaita and Hindu Masters in India.

She spends much of her time in Prashanti Nilayam, south India, where her Guru, Bhagawan Sri Sathya Sai Baba resides.

You can contact Mynavati by email at:
Mynavati27@hotmail.com

Contents

Acknowledgements

Forty-nine Days was written and then shelved for more than a year. When I returned to look at it, I was inspired to re-write it. Really, it began to write itself and I am in no doubt that this was due to the blessings and inspiration of my beloved Guru, Sri Sathya Sai Baba. I owe everything I do to His grace. Swami, I lay this book at Your Sweet Lotus Feet in deepest loving gratitude.

I thank my son Craig, for asking me to write the book so that the people who read it can meet the death of a loved one in a loving and healing way. Thank you too Craig for the wonderful cover design and layout.

I thank Manizeh Sait for believing in Forty-nine Days when I had given up. It is due to Manizeh that I took it off the shelf and gave it a second chance. It is due to her generosity and deep kindness that it has been published.

I thank Sally Allen for helping me with the first run. She gave a lot of effort and assistance in proofing the first manuscript and in helping me cut away what was not essential. Her tremendous efforts gave me the groundwork for the re-write.

I thank Susannah Carrington, Lesley Shatwell, Amanda Wright, Dinah VanSwol-Jarvis, Mary and Charles Simpson, Sally Allen and Mellen-Thomas Benedict for sharing their heart-opening and deeply inspiring personal stories.

I thank all the friends and well-wishers who sent me stories that were not finally included in the book.

I thank my family who are always there for me.

I am deeply grateful to you all. May you all be blessed.

Mynavati

Foreword

The author of this book 'Forty-nine Days', looks at human existence as the journey we have embarked on, to arrive at a point when consciousness awakens us to the Truth that we and all that exists is Love. This deep awareness that comes with this awakening very often awaits opportunities like pain and sorrow caused by separation or loss to bring home this Truth.

All such experiences are in reality a preparation for this empowering transformation not only in us but also in those separated from us and in those existing in their disembodied state, when we realize that ' True Love cannot die regardless of time and space'

We need to Transform. Transformation is the power of unconditional Love in action. It is this unconditional love that gives us the courage to confront our fears, sit with all our pains, admit our frailties, set aside all our guilt and allow us to forgive ourselves, and gradually experience the moment-to-moment dying of our old Self to make way for the new Self - the greater the death the greater the rebirth into the new beginning. The biggest fear we have is the fear of death which actually stems from ignorance and our fears of the unknown.

No Transformation can take place when there is fear - especially fear of death. In the absence of unconditional love no transformation takes place. It is a journey into Self discovery where we find that we are LOVE itself and each of us come by this Truth in our own way.

Manizeh Sait -
The School of Ancient Wisdom

Introduction

'Life is eternally stalked by death.
But man does not like to hear this.
It is considered bad luck to even hear the word;
even though every living thing is, every moment,
proceeding nearer and nearer to that event.
When you are intent upon a journey,
after you purchase your ticket and board the train -
whether you sit quietly, lie down, read or meditate,
the train will take you to the destination.
So too, at birth each living thing has received a ticket
to the event of death and is now on the journey.
Whatever your struggles or precautions,
the place has to be reached some day.
Whatever else may be uncertain in this world -
death is certain.
It is impossible to change the law.'

Sri Sathya Sai Baba

When you experience the death of someone near and dear, you are confronted with a momentous event in your life. You are faced not only with the loss of your loved one, but also with your own inevitable death. This juxaposition catapults you into an emotionally heightened and raw state and at times will feel painfully overwhelming. Your departed loved one too, will face a similar emotional crisis. You will experience this journey together, even though physically apart. Believe in this, for in spite of the apparent finality of your separation, you can in Truth never be separated. Love bonds us. Love connects us. Love unites us. Death has no final power in the face of true Love. In Love, we are joined and affected by one another forever.

From this view, the death of a dear one may be painfully experienced, but need not result in crisis. Through the deep fusion of our heart-connection we find the true meaning to life. We experience the journey of the opening of the heart - The Holy Grail - the journey of Love Itself. The aim of true Love is not a deepening entrenchment of attachment that results in misery when the other is no longer there. True devotion between two people, is the helping of one another in their quests towards God and freedom with the knowledge that in actuality there is no other. There is only Love. **Sri Sathya Sai Baba** declares,

'Cherish Love... All are one... There is only one God, the Supreme Divinity that is present in all beings and permeates the entire cosmos. The Divine is present in every atom. Everything is composed of energy and matter... In every human being this divine energy is present.'

Give thanks that you have been given the opportunity to Love, at the same time, knowing that your Loved one is in essence at one with yourself and all that is. Feel gratitude that your deep Love will take you to the frontiers of illusion and

Truth and will finally lead you over the border to Liberation - to the realization of the Quest of your soul and the reason and meaning of your birth and life.

'The inner meaning of life does not readily reveal itself;
it must be searched for.
Such a search is the Quest.
When a man begins to seek out his real nature,
to find the truth of his real being,
he begins to follow the Quest.'

Paul Brunton

Forty-nine Days honours the great journey, the Quest of your soul, while supporting you through the vulnerable process of coming to terms with your very human loss. During this time, you will learn how to help your beloved as well as yourself. Forty-nine Days is a positive companion - a friend to help you both during this crucial transition. The intrinsic belief of this book is that death is not the end. Death is embraced as the beginning of something unknown and mysterious and filled with promise - a journey into possibilities and hope through the power of your Love.

Life is unfathomable and sometimes frightening. Not only that, but it can be thought of as never-ending. Birth, life death, rebirth, death... What is this great epic asking of us? The preciousness of a human life is that it has the consciousness to know and realize God. Consciousness does not die when we stop breathing. Consciousness, Love, goes on. It becomes fuller, greater as it journeys through life and death and from birth to rebirth until such time it becomes completely at One with Itself.

Forty-nine Days celebrates the connection of Love in life and death, but it does not deny the terrible suffering of loss. If you include the hurt, something greater than you can imagine will emerge. Something, that goes beyond the pain and which can never be harmed by anything or anyone. And so, you are encouraged to grieve and to enter the world of loss. You are given permission to fully feel and connect with the immensity of what is happening. You will be inspired to connect deeply with your loved one in many ways. In this, both your feelings can be fully met. Without this allowing, you can never move on.

Why forty-nine days for this vigil? There is more than one reason why I chose this period of time. Seven weeks seemed right as the focus for this intense period of initial adjustment and grieving. Any less would have been too short and any more would have felt unmanageably long for the purposes of the book. But Forty-nine Days is written in a way that you can re-read chapters again and again for as long as you need and want to.

This book is a guide, as well as an inspiration. You do not need to read it from beginning to end - at least not initially. When coping with bereavement it is often too difficult to concentrate on reading a book in this way. And so, you can simply open it at any page and receive inspiration, comfort or an answer to a question. You can also read passages to your loved one. There is no doubt that they will hear you.

The timing of Forty-nine Days was influenced by one of

the greatest treatises on death and the inward journey, The Tibetan Book of the Dead. In this ancient and profound book it is taught how the deceased does not normally remain in the in-between world, the Bardo, for longer than forty-nine days after which time, they are reborn. During this span of time the one who has died has experiences which give them the opportunity for total freedom or a good rebirth.

I received Initiation into the teachings of The Tibetan Book of the Dead - the Bardo Teachings, while living in the Himalayas in 1993-95 however this book does not belong to Tibetan Buddhism or any other philosophy or religion. It draws inspirationally from many different paths, teachings and teachers. To name a few, first and foremost, the teachings of my Guru, Sri Sathya Sai Baba, who is the inspiration of my work and all that I do, The Ancient Scriptures of the Vedas and Puranas, in particular, the Garuda Purana and the Katha Upanishad, The Christian Bible and inspiring thoughts and words from the mystics and poets of many different ages and cultures. The thread that runs through all is the concept of One-ness (Advaita) - there is no you and I. There is only One and it's nature is Love.

The Divine words and names of Jesus, The Buddha, Allah, the Guru, Truth, God, Oneness, Wholeness, Light and Love are interchangeable and are One. It is up to the reader to choose which Divine name and form they feel most connected to and to use this form no matter what other form they are reading about.

Forty-nine is the number of Revolution in the I Ching, the ancient, wise Chinese Book of Changes. The book of Changes tells us how change is a constant, permanent force, which pervades everything and everywhere. Life and death too are subject to change. They are not static. Death is a revolution of the heart. Love is a revolution. Love is the Divine Dance. Love is the beginning and the end. Love is God.

Although Forty-nine Days is presented as a companion for those who have experienced a loss through death there are many kinds of loss, which are also final. People suffer loss though divorce or separation from their beloved. Children leave their parents never to return. A parent will abandon a child never to be seen again. This book can be used as a helping support for anyone who undergoes grief through the loss of a loved one. Intentionally different kinds of relationships, of husband and wife, mother and child and friends are not highlighted. The beloved and Love belong to the Universal Heart and not to particular forms of relationship.

Forty-nine Days is an exploration. It does not limit you to supposed definite conclusions about how, what and where. How can it do so, when The Truth is the greatest mystery? What matters here is the connection between two hearts and how this deep bond can awaken you to the Truth of your Self - that you and all that exists, is Love and Love alone. Without doubt True Love cannot die, regardless of time and space. I pray that through the union of your Love, you and all those who have gone before you and who will come after you, find freedom, peace and true happiness during this precious and intense time.

Mynavati

forty-nine days

Prelude

A First-Hand Experience

'At the moment of death
you will see what your whole life's work
was preparing you to do.'

Ram Dass

Death and I met when I drowned as a child. This was my first encounter of a near death experience. I had some more as a teenager and adult. What these brushes with death gave me was a deep respect for the preciousness of every moment of every life in all creation. I feel sometimes that it is as though we all hang to life by a very fine thread. But the thread is Divine, and when it is not our time to leave our body, nothing and no-one can break it.

The encounters with death also blessed me with a deep respect for the great mystery of death and the on-going journey. They proved to me without any doubt that we are more than the body and that death is not the end - that, in a body or not, our consciousness relentlessly continues in expansion towards Oneness with God.

This first near death experience jolted me into life. This test run offered my young self a glimpse of how we are held by a wisdom and power that is greater than life and death. I have come to accept this great power as Love Itself. This Love is not external to us. It is the very essence of us and everything ad everyone. It is written in the Garuda Purana, 'O Garuda! Exactly as the time of death, a man develops divine vision like the gods.' This was my experience. At my moment of death I met the Divine, in the form of Compassion.

I was nine years old. Until that time I had been ambivalent about being alive. From birth I did not sleep. While the rest of the world slept when it was dark and quiet I would lie awake with my thoughts and a deep sense of isolation. This made me feel separate from the world I had been born into.

An instinctive wisdom turned me to God as God felt very real to me, more real than anything or anyone I experienced in Life. Who else could I turn to during those dark, lonely nights? The turning became a longing for a deeper union. I have memories from the age of three, sitting up in bed praying to God, pleading with Him to take me home. Each morning as the sun rose, I was devastated that I was still sitting on my bed. As I grew older and life beckoned with more experiences, the despair lessened, but the yearning to be somewhere else, where I thought God was, continued to burn deep within me.

Six years later I stood by the edge of a swimming pool looking into the clear still water. My parents had allowed me to go to the local swimming baths with some neighbouring children. I was so excited never having been to a swimming pool before that I was the first to change into my swimsuit and I ran to the edge of the pool still wearing white ankle-socks, spectacles and wristwatch.

As I looked into the water there was no knowing how deep it was. I knew that swimming pools had a shallow end and a deep end but I did not know which end was which. For some strange, inexplicable reason, I had no intention of waiting to find out. A thought came "Just jump!" More thoughts came. "If it is the shallow end you will land on your feet and if it is the deep end you will start swimming and if you cannot swim it will be okay because you will go "home". I'd never had a swimming lesson in my life.

I jumped into the deep end. I clearly remember how my body felt as it entered the water. Time went into slow motion as I slowly sank to the bottom. I bounced back up to the surface. I took a deep breath but could not swim. I had no idea how to and so I quickly sank again. My feet hit the bottom of the slippery pool and catapulted me once more to the surface. I took a deep gulp of air. I tried to get someone's attention. I waved, but the movement made me go under even more quickly. This happened a few times, until I was unable to rise again. I found myself sitting on the tiled floor of the pool as I watched swimmers above me quietly gliding past, completely oblivious of me.

I sat there, defeated and exhausted. Everything around me began to dissolve and grow lighter. I felt that I was no longer in my body and I was aware of a floating, expansive feeling. Two luminous scenes opened up in either side of my vision like two bright panoramic cinema scenes. On the left I saw my mother and father opening the door to a policeman who was telling them that their only child had drowned. On the right I saw myself running towards them as I returned from the swimming baths. Through the heart, my consciousness was tangibly pulled to the left where my mother was now collapsing with grief and my father's face was white and distraught...

My heart felt as though it was bursting as I watched their pain. My heart opened. It was a tangible feeling. I wanted them to be happy. I wanted them to be the happy mum and dad in the scene where I was running towards them. My heart made a choice.

I came to, with water pouring out of my mouth as I lay on the edge of the poolside being resuscitated. Clearly it was not my time to go home. And, finally, it was the first time in my young life that I felt it was okay to stay.

This act of dying gave me a glimpse of the power of Divine Love and of what I now believe is the true purpose of life. Life is not for self but for the compassion of all including oneself. It is the journey of the opening of the heart. The experience also took away any possible fear of death. Death is the companion of life and is to be respected. But it need not be feared. Indeed, death is the porthole to the naked and unadulterated heart where one can unite with Love Itself.

I have no doubt that when someone dies they are guided, held and cared for by Love as they continue their existence in their own beautiful and unique way.

* * *

'A human being is a part of a whole, called by us 'universe,'
a part limited in time and space.
He experiences himself, his thoughts and feelings as
something separated from the rest...
a kind of optical delusion of his consciousness.
This delusion is a kind of prison for us, restricting us
to our personal desires and to affection for a few persons
nearest to us. Our task must be to free ourselves
from this prison by widening our circle of compassion
to embrace all living creatures
and the whole of nature in its beauty.'

Albert Einstein

★ ★ ★

forty-nine days

Love and Death

Chapter 1

Reflections

Days One to Three

'Death is not extinguishing the light;
it is putting out the lamp
because the dawn has come.'

Rabindranath Tagore

Today a part of you has died. For when you lose someone you love, a piece of you is severed too. Humans are not solitary beings. We need to feel a connection with others to enter the world of our hearts and to fulfil our deep and complex loving nature. We need to feel love and to experience how it is to be loved. There is a price we pay for this unique and marvellous richness of interdependence. Experiencing the intensity of relationship, the joy of belonging opens one to the vulnerability and pain of loss. But when you really Love, and continue to Love, you gain something precious that can never be taken from you, not even by the Lord of Death.

* * *

'Ever has it been that Love knows not its own depth
until the hour of separation.'

Kahlil Gibran

* * *

Something has happened in your heart, something has awakened in your being - your souls have touched one another. Rejoice! Because in your coming together, neither of you will ever be the same again. Your Love opened one another's hearts. Death in the temporary world can never erase the truth of Love that constantly shines from the permanent and eternal Heart. You will always Love one another. You are in Truth one Heart. There is no beloved and no lover. There is no mother and child. There is no husband and wife. There is Love alone.

* * *

'Love is neither personal nor impersonal.
Love is Love,
not to be defined or described by the mind
as exclusive or inclusive.
Love is its own eternity;
it is the real,
the supreme,
the immeasurable.'

J. Krishnamurti

★ ★ ★

What is this Love, that made Jesus die on the cross for others, which made Gautama Buddha in his previous incarnation, offer his young healthy body to a hunger-dying tiger and her cubs... The same Love, that flowed through Mother Theresa like a river as she gave her body and life to loving the poor, the sick, the dying, and the filthy, unwanted lepers and beggars of Calcutta. This Love is a very special kind of Love. It is real Love. It is authentic because it is completely selfless. It is Godly Love... The seeds of this Love are deep within you. They cannot be otherwise, because this Love is the spiritual force of you. It is what you have been searching for all your life and what you found deep in your beloved's eyes.

This is the Love that you need to claim for your sake and for the sake of your loved one. This Love heals and makes whole. It is the Love that survives death.

★ ★ ★

There is another kind of love, which does not survive at all. You have to find this love within you and destroy it. Otherwise it will destroy you. It can never give you what you really need and want. Love is a word that is used so casually and frequently nowadays. But most people do not know what they are really talking about. We grow up hearing phrases like *love makes the world go around*. We feel that we must love. We are encouraged to love things, people, beloveds, but only when they are how we want them to be. If they are not as we think they should be, we are encouraged to toss them away. We celebrate falling in love. The whole world loves a lover. But when this kind of love dies, as it has to, we become hurt, cynical, disillusioned, depressed or so distraught that we are unable to survive.

This is the love of attachment and delusion. It is based on need and possession. It cannot last for it is related to the mortal and the temporary. If the object of your love dies, you will feel like dying too. If the object of your love leaves you, you will want to kill the love you have felt.

★ ★ ★

I was a trainee nurse when I was a youth. One evening when I was on night duty, a young man, in his mid-thirties was rushed into the ward. He was unconscious and in a critical condition. He was haemorrhaging inside. We tried everything to save him. But he died within a few hours. It was shocking to see such a young, externally healthy looking man die so quickly. His wife was inconsolable. She collapsed and was admitted to a ward upstairs. She never left the hospital. She died within one week from a broken heart.

I felt deeply for these two vital people who died so tragically and without warning. One day, they were well and happy and on the next, catastrophe had struck and they were dead. I tried to understand the young woman's grief - a grief so immense she could not live without her husband. Was this really necessary, I kept asking myself? How could she not accept what had happened and continue to live the rest of her life? I wondered. Who knows what could have been ahead for her. But, her life was so inextricably merged with the love she had for her husband, that when he died, it was not possible for her to continue.

★ ★ ★

As I matured, there were times I experienced life so painfully that I could barely face it. I came to grief very much like the young woman in the hospital who had died of a broken heart all those years before. I loved the object of my love so much that I thought I would die when he disappeared from my life. Many times, I did not want to live. But, I had to go on, because I had enough grace to know that suicide was not the answer.

But, one night as I lay in a hotel room in Bangalore, I reached breaking point. My husband, my home in Kerala, my belongings, my life as I knew it, had been taken away from me as though overnight. I was smashed into tiny pieces. I could not put myself together again no matter how I tried. I was barely able to function.

I had been surviving in Puttaparthi, where Sai Baba resides, but had to go to Bangalore for a few nights to attend to some matters. Around that time, a Nadi reader (1) had told me that when it was my time to die it would be my choice and I would be able leave my body at will. As I lay there, looking up at the dirty fan twirling round on the ceiling of the rather dark, dingy hotel room, I thought that there could be no better time than now.

Grief is such a strong anguish that it envelops and colours your entire world. When it becomes tarnished by despair and egocentricity it eclipses your heart and makes you self-centred and selfish. I remembered my son in Ireland and his family, my grandchildren, my mother in Scotland... Friends... I told myself that they were all living happy, good lives, and that I was not an integral part of their lives anymore. I told myself that although they would be initially shocked at my passing, they would all get over it pretty quickly and be alright. It was easy to believe the lies. They suited my purpose. The truth is that they would have been devastated, but in my blind despair, I could not comprehend this. I decided to die there and then. I believed I could will myself to leave my body. This was different from suicide I argued with my conscience convincingly. This was natural. This was just my time!

I had no fear of death - only of living. With immense determination I asked my life force to leave my body. After some time, I was aware of energy moving from areas of my body and gathering at a central point. Wonderful I thought. It's working! It was coming together like a vortex and leaving through the Heart Chakra. This was not one of the best of signs. It's much better if the energy leaves through the Crown Chakra. (2) It meant that I would be reborn. But that did not matter. What mattered was that I left the life I was in. I began to feel weak and drift...

Immediately, Sai Baba was by my side, looking into my eyes intently "Are you alright?" He questioned. I refused to answer Him. I felt I knew what He was trying to do. He was trying to engage me. He wanted to distract me from my aim. He lightly moved around me, like a stalking panther, not taking his eyes from my eyes, "Are you alright?" He said again coming even closer to my face. I was determined to remain resolute. I was not going to play.

But something deep within me could not resist Him because I found myself travelling with Him. I was out of my body but I knew I was not dead. This was not what I had planned but I could not stop it. We reached a contained space which had boundaries that were invisible to me. But, I could feel them. It was like a reception room. People were sitting, waiting for Swami (Sai Baba). I knew they could not see me. They animatedly talked with Swami while I sat by the side of His left leg. "How did this happen. How did I get here," I asked myself crossly. Swami was giving the people a wonderful interview. They were so excited to see Him and they were talking and laughing. He was manifesting items of jewellery and handing them round. I continued to try not to engage. I refused to look at them.

There was a circular glass-topped table in front of Swami placed between Him and the group. I could not see it but I knew it was there. Spontaneously, in spite of myself, I moved my right hand in a circular motion as Swami does when He divinely manifests an object. A ring manifested between my fingers. I reached under the table and placed it on Swami's ring finger as His hand lay on His lap. He immediately looked at me. There was joy, a look of triumph in his eyes. "Got you.' They said. I melted as He looked at me so lovingly, as a father looks at His child when they have done something very special and wonderful. He looked so proud, so pleased...

I came to on my bed in absolute bliss. I knew that what I had experienced was not a dream. It was a Divine happening. My life slowly changed from then on. I went back to Puttaparthi and a short while later, Swami told me, "Stay. I will look after you." I gradually became more peaceful and content.

Godly Love is expansive and free. And Swami taught me the most wonderful lesson - that regardless of how blind the mind is, Love is eternally present. In the spontaneous creation of the ring, Sai Baba proved to me how Divinity is One. At that moment I was One with Him and Love manifested in the creation of a gift, in the form of a ring.

* * *

'If you have never reached the bottomless depths of despair,
if you have not realised some point in your life
at which you felt completely disintegrated,
then you haven't begun your journey towards God yet.
But immediately upon that disintegration,
when everything you value in life is gone,
there should be a surrender.
The cup of your personality shatters,
and at that moment of shattering
you surrender your will completely to the unknown,
whoever the unknown is,
and right there, by that very act,
you have found the perfection that is God.'

Pandit Usharbudh Arya

I am so grateful to have known a Love that was so karmic (3) and filled with overwhelming attachment that it almost extinguished me. It was my means to disintegration and surrender. I am grateful that I survived to tell the tale. The experience taught me how narrow and destructive a love with such attachment is.

As the months and years passed, I was blessed with the help of Divine Grace through Sai Baba to continue my life in openness. I did not shut down in bitterness, as I know I could have done. With His help, my heart stayed open. My attachments burned in the fire of Reality and sacrifice. It was painful for a very long time. Then something wonderful happened. My heart transformed. I understood on a level that I could not comprehend before, that I could not own anything or anyone, ever. No one can. It is an illusion when we think that we do. I understood how my true happiness did not, could not, depend on another, being there for me. I realised that this kind of attachment has nothing to do with Love at all. In fact, it conceals Love.

★ ★ ★

Love is about loving without expectation of any return. It is praying that the other finds peace and happiness, even if this means without you. It is the respect of another's life, death and journey.

Love has nothing to do with belonging or loss. One Loves for Love's own sake. One Loves because one cannot help doing so. And the wonderful thing you will discover is that Love cannot be exclusive. It is Divine. Divine means not mine!

Love, really means loving God, and seeing how everything and everyone is God. Love is wishing for the happiness and peace for all as well as the beloved. This is when you really begin to get to know Love. When you feel the immensity of gratitude for having the experience of loving someone so much that it takes you beyond yourself. When you touch this Love deep within you, your Love survives beyond Death itself.

* * *

'In this worldly life,
Love is manifesting in several forms
such as the Love between mother and son,
husband and wife, and between relatives.
This Love based on physical relationships arises
out of selfish motives and self-interest.
But the Love of the Divine is devoid of any trace
of self-interest. It is Love for the sake of Love alone.
This is called Bhakti or devotion.
One characteristic of this Love is to give and not to receive.
Secondly Love knows no fear.
Thirdly, it is only for Love' sake and not for selfish motive.
All these three angles of Love jointly connote surrender.
When one revels in this attitude of surrender one
experiences the bliss of the Divine.
For this, the prime requisite is forgiveness.'

Sri Sathya Sai Baba

* * *

Many years ago, one of my Spritual Teacher's instructed me to remember my impending death as I awoke each morning, with the awareness that this may be my last day. As I continued with my practice, I realized how death can strike at any moment and how I needed to be prepared now. Not only for my own death but also for the death of those I knew and loved. This daily awareness has made my life all the sweeter and deeper. It brought home to me how everyone is uniquely precious and mortal, including myself. It made me appreciate the experience of life in a way I could not have done so before.

* * *

Death strips us of the clichés and the so-called right formulas. It crashes the mind of its solid, fixed ideas. If you wish to, face yourself each day in the mirror of death. You will see yourself very clearly - much more clearly than before. If you so desire, you will see your attachments laid bare. Whatever you find, do not judge yourself. Be kind to yourself. Be glad that you have this time of Grace to see what imprisons you. You have the choice to let them go. When they die, you will see that what remain is the immensity of Love alone.

* * *

Like a skilled surgeon, let your pain cut away your attachments. Try not to quickly stitch up the open wounds. Allow the pure air of Consciousness pentrate the sores and heal them. Heal permanently into freedom.

* * *

All you need is Faith. Faith in the belief that there is a Higher Power one can surrender to, which knows what is best for you, your loved one and for all concerned. Faith is not something that can be acquired. It is an attribute of your soul. Faith is Divine. You do not need to worry about finding it, for you can never be without it. Without faith you cannot live. Without faith you cannot die. Without faith there is no existence.

★ ★ ★

'When one has faith in the ways of the Lord
And abides by the will of the Lord,
The Lord can be understood and experienced.'

Sri Sathya Sai Baba

★ ★ ★

During these crucial days you have the choice to journey with your beloved towards limitless Peace and Eternal Love. You can choose to spend your time in despair, or you can use the precious moments of your life to explore the possibility of a greater hope and freedom. Yes, include your grief and do not hold back... Grief is not the same as despair. Despair is without hope. Despair does not help you. It only suffocates you and your potential. Grief is an honourable expression of sorrow and pain. Do not pretend and repress. But as you cry and deeply feel the sadness, be aware too of the opportunity for momentous change - be aware of remaining open in your heart. Stay receptive to the idea of limitless possibilities and the promise of release, spiritual maturity and peace.

* * *

Remind yourself that nothing lasts - not even the stars. The moon, the earth, the sun, the very Universe… all will vanish one day. Be grateful for what you have had and what you are given. Be honest about your grief. Be honest about the depth of your pain. Be honest about the magnitude of death and the exprience of life. Honesty clears the road to recovery. Affirm, "I was fortunate to have met you. I was blessed to share this part of my life with you. I would not be who I am now without having had this rare and momentous time with you. Oh my dear, I Love you and I want you to be happy and free. I Love you enough to want both of us to be happy and free."

* * *

'Mourning is not forgetting…
It is an undoing.
Every minute tie has to be untied
and something permanent and valuable recovered
and assimilated from the dust.'

Margery Allingham

* * *

No one can really understand what you are feeling, what you are going through. In this experience of loss, you and everyone else is alone. One's experience and emotions are individual and unique. But remember that others can empathise with you. Others too will experience this fate. Death, impermanence, is the penalty we pay for life. Nothing and no one escapes this fact. Death is as natural as life itself. Remember too, that no matter how alone and separate from others you may feel, God is within you, around you, above you, before you, behind you and below you. God is everywhere with you. God is wherever you are. God is everything and everyone. God is your eternal and loyal friend.

* * *

'Abide with me, fast falls the eventide;
The darkness deepens, Lord with me abide!
When other helpers fail and comforts flee,
help of the helpless,
O abide with me...
I need Thy presence every passing hour;
What but Thy grace can foil the tempter's power?
Who, like Thyself, my guide and stay can be?
Through cloud and sunshine,
Lord, abide with me.'

Henry Francis Lyte (1793-1847)

* * *

Let today be the beginning of the quest to find the jewel of your heart. You can ask, "What is the greatest Truth I can realize in this drama of Love, life and death that surrounds me?" Something is being asked of you beyond your immediate feelings and senses - beyond even the relationship you had with your dear one. Now you are confronted with the truth of life. Everything and everyone will cease to be. Ask what is the deepest meaning and healing for you as you are faced with the impact of your beloved's death? Do not stop questioning until you receive answers that satisfy you.

★ ★ ★

'I wonder if you have ever known what Love is?
Because I think death and Love walk together.
Death, Love, and life are one and the same.
But we have divided life, as we have divided the earth.
We talk of Love as being either carnal or spiritual and have
set a battle going between the sacred and the profane.
We have divided what Love is from what Love should be,
so we never know what Love is.
Love, surely, is a total feeling that is not sentimental
and in which there is no sense of separation.
It is complete purity of feeling without the separative
fragmenting quality of the intellect. Love has no sense of
continuity. Where there is a sense of continuity, Love is
already dead, and it smells of yesterday, with all its ugly
memories, quarrels, brutalities. To Love, one must die.'

J Krishnamurti

★ ★ ★

The experience of death is natural. If it is natural how can it be bad? Death is a natural part of the process of life. Everyone who is born will die. We are dying all the time. Birth is as natural as death but do we grieve when a baby is born? The baby dies from the womb. Yet we rejoice as it enters its new existence in our world. In the same way, the Angels and Divine beings rejoice as your beloved leaves this sphere and joins with them.

Go beyond the limitations and parameters of your mind. There is no better time than now.

★ ★ ★

Death is Universal

Sogyal Rinpoche tells the story of Krisha Gotami who lived in the time of the Buddha. Her young child died and she was completely grief stricken. She could not accept it. Carrying her dead child, she searched throughout her village, wailing and hoping to find someone who could restore her baby to life.

A wise man told her that the Buddha was in the area and that he had the power to restore life. She went to the Buddha and placing the dead child at his feet, pleaded with him to bring her child back to life. The Buddha told her that he would bring the infant back from the dead if she brought him mustard seeds from any house in the local village in which a death had not occurred.

Krishna Gotami searched the entire village and its surroundings. She knocked on every door and met with the same answer. All had experienced the death of a dear one. She was unable to find any home where death had not occurred.

Krisha Gotami sat down, weary with her search, consoling her grief stricken face between her hands. She realized that suffering the death of a loved one is universal. What she was going through was no different from that of all sentient beings in the world. This was the nature of life.

Krisha Gotami finally accepted what had happened to her child. She dedicated the remainder of her life towards spiritual practice in preparation for her own death. This was the great grace the Buddha bestowed upon her.

★　★　★

And what of your beloved? In this time of quiet, your heart may ask, "Where are they now? Are there really such places as Heaven and Hell? Is there really life beyond death?" You may be afraid that all those who believe in and teach Eternal Life are mistaken. In times of fear, you may be troubled that there is no other home they can go to. It is at these times that you must grasp faith. Faith is not something outside you. It is an intrinsic part of your soul. Remember all the great teachers and beings who have walked the earth who have told us that there is in fact no death. That, there is only the death of the body. Can they all be wrong? Have trust. Have faith.

★　★　★

'I remember watching a five-year-old boy
draw a picture in an effort to explain to his mother
how pleasant his death experience had been.
First he drew a brightly coloured castle and said,
"This is where God lives."
Then he added a brilliant star.
"When I saw the star,
it said, "Welcome home."

Elisabeth Kubler-Ross

* * *

The Language of Love

This is a true story of a young Jewish boy and his father, set in the 20th century. It is told by **Gregg Braden** in a series of CD's called **The Lost Language of God**. Gregg tells us that he cannot remember when he first heard the story or who told him. But, it left a lasting impression on him and he never forgot it. It has had the same effect on me. It is a beautiful, poignant account of how Love cannot die, even in the shroud of apparent separation and death.

The story is of a young boy, who begins to question the Jewish traditions he has been raised in, their validity and what they mean to him in his life. His father takes the boy's questioning very personally and is offended. They argue. The boy tells his father that although he has been raised in the Hebrew tradition, he needs to go out into the world and test the teachings for himself. That it is only by doing this that he can understand whether the traditions hold true for him and his life. The father tells the boy that if he turns his back on the traditions he has been raised in, from then on he will no longer be his son.

The boy is saddened, but reiterates to his father that regardless of how his father feels, he needs to leave his home to find out what is valid for him and his life. He soon leaves the United States and embarks on travelling the world.

But, throughout his travels the boy does not forget his past and the teachings and upbringing he has received. He tests them and observes how they serve his life and interactions with others. He finally arrives in Europe, meets a girl, falls in love, marries and settles down to a happy, contented life.

Years go by in which the young man has no contact with his father. One day, while sitting in a coffee bar, an old friend from America walks in. They have not seen one another since he left the States years before. They are very happy to meet after so long, but the first thing that his friend tells him is how sorry he is to hear about the death of his father. The young man had no idea that his father had died. He is shocked. He immediately returns to the States. When he speaks with family and friends in his old neighbourhood he discovers a revelation. He finds out that even though they had no contact, his father had never forgotten him. In fact, he discovers that his father spoke about him incessantly, of how proud he was of his son having the strength and the courage to go out into the world and find his own way.

This knowledge and the connection he feels with his father brings the boy closer to the roots of his Hebrew tradition, the Jewish faith. He makes a commitment to go to the place where it all began and he soon finds himself in Jerusalem at the famous Wailing Wall where people of his tradition perform their prayers on a daily basis. This unique and amazing centuries old wall is made of very ancient stone blocks, held with mortar. Where the mortar has fallen out over time, one can find tiny pieces of paper and scraps of cloth rolled up and stuffed in all the little crevices, nooks and crannies.

Each one of the pieces of cloth and bits of paper contains a prayer that someone has inscribed. In the tradition of the young man's roots, he also decides to inscribe a prayer honouring the relationship with his father. As he scans the wall with his eyes, searching for just the right place where he can leave his prayer, a prayer that someone else had placed before him, suddenly drops out at his feet. He bends to pick it up with the intention of placing the small piece of paper back in the wall. But something stops him. The handwriting is familiar. The young man looks at the prayer more closely. It is like the handwriting of his father. How can this be? He opens the prayer and what he finds is that it is indeed his father's handwriting. Before his father died, he too had journeyed to exactly the same place and had placed a prayer in the wall giving thanks for his relationship with his son and the beauty that his son had brought into his life.

In this potent moment the young man is faced with the awesome awareness that even though his father is no longer in this world, there is still a powerful connection between them, there is still communication. There is still Love.

★ ★ ★

'I hold it true, what'er befall;
I feel it, when I sorrow most;
'Tis better to have Loved and lost,
than never to have Loved at all.'

Alfred Lord Tennyson

* * *

Remember at all times that inherent in the apparent destruction of death and loss, Divine Love is at work. As you let go the limitations of your usual boundaries, today and each day during the next forty-nine days, you will have an opportunity to experience Oneness with The Creator and the Divine View. The sacrifice for this deepening awareness is the journey of loss you have embarked upon and will continue to travel until you assimilate a new way, a new meaning, a new life emerging within you that would not have been possible before.

* * *

'Reality is merely an illusion,
albeit a very persistent one.'

Albert Einstein

* * *

'Imagine a house with four walls and a roof.
If the house burns down, the walls and the roof collapse.
But the space inside isn't affected.
You can hire an architect to design a new house, and after
you build it, the space inside still hasn't been affected.
By building a house you are only dividing unbounded space
into inside and outside. This division is an illusion.
The ancient sages said that your body is like that house.
It's built at birth and burns down when you die,
yet the Akasha, or soul space, remains unchanged;
it remains unbounded.'

Deepak Chopra

* * *

The Ancient teachings of the East, tell us that we are deluded if we think that this world and all that we see is real. They tell us that life is an illusion - a dream from which we will awaken. They teach that there is no real birth and death. There is only the illusion that we have been born and that we die. But what does this really mean and how can these teachings comfort us in times of loss, unless we really understand their meaning?

Here is a wonderful ancient story set in the time of Lord Krishna about Maya (Illusion of our relative world). Lord Krishna was an Avatar (manifested God in form) who lived approximately 5000 years ago. Narada is the travelling Divine sage, a great devotee of the Lord, with the ability to visit distant worlds or planets.

Krishna's Maya

Once the Rishi Narada came to Sri Krishna and said "My Lord, what actually is this Maya of yours?"

"Maya?" said Krishna, "All right, come for a walk with me!" They walked for a long time. When a village came into sight, Krishna said, "I'm thirsty. Fetch me a glass of water." Narada went into the village, while Krishna waited for him.

Narada asked for water at the first house he came to. The housewife who came to the door, called to her beautiful daughter to fetch the water. The girl and Narada's eyes met. He could barely take his eyes from her. He was infatuated at first sight.

When she returned with the water, the mother, aware of a great opportunity to marry her daughter to a very presentable young man, said to him, "Why don't you marry my daughter?" Narada, totally enchanted with the lovely girl, readily agreed.

They got married and had two children, a son and a daughter, and lived a very happy and contented life. All went well until one day torrential rains caused a flood. The water penetrated their house and continued to rise. It kept on rising until finally Narada and his family were forced onto the roof. Still the water rose and rose. At last Narada had to try to hold onto his entire family in order to keep them from being swept away. His mother-in-law was now quite old. She could not hold on. She lost her grip and quickly drowned.

Narada thought, "She was old and near death anyhow! At

least I have the rest of my family." But very soon, his daughter was pulled away by the force of the water and disappeared. He was shocked as he saw her body carried away by the flood. He thought, "My daughter is gone but at least my son is still alive!" But, no sooner than the thought came into his mind, his son was pulled away by the fierce current and he too drowned.

Narada was greatly distressed. He clasped his beautiful wife to him, and consoled himself thinking, "As long as I have my wife, I may have other children." But then his wife too was swept away.

He himself could not stay afloat. Gasping for breath and about to give up, he found himself standing again next to Krishna, still panting. Krishna looked at him and calmly said, "What is the matter with you. Where is my glass of water?"

Narada replied, "Lord, now I know what your Maya is."

Adapted from a story told by Shree Anandamayee Ma

* * *

Through the deep connection of Narada's Love and devotion for Krishna, he was able to wake-up from illusion and re-unite with Krishna - with God and Truth. As you travel through these days, leave your doubts behind. Commit to journey with the hope and belief that you can go beyond the illusion of time, form and space. Read the great teachings contained in The Holy Bible, The Tibetan Book of the Dead, the Indian Vedic literature and any other great spiritual teachings you feel drawn to. Take from them what feels good for you. They will help to strengthen your resolve of faith. They not only teach that death is not the end, but some give us concise details of the stages the deceased passes through when the body is left behind and of the Afterlife. (4)

★ ★ ★

Imagine that your loved one's consciousness is resting, yet still hovering near to their body. What do you feel that they need most from you at this time - tears, distress, anguish or acceptance and even happiness at this, their new birth? Consider that they are influenced by your thoughts, actions and reactions. Be aware that because of the power of your bonding with one another, that their ability to go forward is also dependant on how you feel at this crucial time.

★ ★ ★

Visualize that at this very moment your beloved is merging with God. Here there is total freedom and peace from further suffering. Let this be your blessing. Throughout your day, visualise this scene as vividly as you can. Your loved one will be aware of your visual prayer and this will help them find the Light of God, wherever they are and however they feel.

★ ★ ★

'Approaching death and death itself,
the dissolution of the physical form,
is always a great opportunity for spiritual realization.
This opportunity is tragically missed most of the time,
since we live in a culture that is almost totally ignorant of
death, as it is almost totally ignorant of anything
that truly matters....
Every portal is a portal of death,
the death of a false self...'

Sri Sathya Sai Baba

* * *

What is spiritual realization you may ask? Sai Baba teaches us that it is not something that can be found through the logic of the mind or through sacrifice or even good deeds. It is not possible through discussion. It can only be found through Love.

Love is all that there is. All the forms and experiences survive because of Love but they are nothing without Love. They cannot exist.

Sai Baba tells us:

'The moments of realisation
are those when all thoughts
or worldly relations,
worldly connections,
worldly ties,
worldly property,

worldly desires,
worldly need
are all metted into God,
into Truth (Love).'

* * *

Make a commitment today to find a quiet place, where you can light a small candle at an appointed hour. You may only have 10 minutes to spare or if you are blessed, perhaps an hour. The amount of time is not crucial. What is important is the commitment of your heart. Such a pledge is more important than margins or boundaries of time.

Within this sacred space, make a crucial connection with your dear one. Here, both of you can obtain more peace than ever imagined. In this place of solace seek tranquillity and hand over your pain to the Divine authority of your choice. Hand over your loved one to the same authority. This representation of God will nourish you as you surrender your burden of loss and pain. Allow yourself to be held. Allow your dear one to be held. Trust in your Love. Trust that Love holds you both.

* * *

Before you go to sleep at night, let us share a prayer with your beloved, as an offering to The Creator and to the Love that holds us always.

Dear One,
on these first nights that you have gone
I pray that you are at peace
and where you belong.
Let us not be so sad -
let us be at Peace.
Let us be happy for this time of sacred space
and the opportunity of Heavenly Grace.

I pray for myself
and for everyone who knew you
who grieve and already miss you.
And so, I grieve,
for this is a fact -
There really will never be another you.

But I remind myself
that you are more than that still body,
And that the purpose of your life was not just me
or anyone else you met here.
You came to grow in Love
to be more Divine
and to be FREE.

I call to all the unseen Angels and helpers
who I know welcomed you.
Let the Great Light shine
through all their guidance.
Wake up, my dear,
the sky is the limit…
you can fly free…

★ ★ ★

Sally's story is of how her mother, as promised, contacts her after death through the power of deep Love and connection.

Janet's Gift

I was living in Colombo, Sri Lanka in 1985. This particular weekend, my husband and I were up country in the lovely tea planting hills. After a relaxed day, we ate an early dinner in the old hotel and went straight to bed.

We must have been asleep by 11p.m. and I should have slept soundly but for no apparent reason, I awoke at approximately 1.30 a.m. and proceeded to remake my side of the bed, smoothing the sheets and blankets and tucking them in, without a thought as to what had woken me or why I was doing it. I then got back into bed and fell fast asleep.

I opened my eyes the following morning to the sun peeking through the curtains and the dream burst into my consciousness, "I had the most beautiful dream of Mummy last night!" I exclaimed to Gordon across the pillow. It was so real, so completely tangible, I was thrilled by the experience and I excitedly described it in every detail.

My Mother was standing on a pavement. She was holding an old fashioned doctor's type bag in her hand and she was wearing a hat and the most beautifully tailored coat. She was standing straight and tall and she was clearly radiant with happiness. I helped her into the back of a car and put the bag at her feet. No words were spoken. It was clear she was going on a journey and she was thrilled to bits about it. I had never seen her looking so glowing, carefree and expectant. It was contagious. This image was a real contrast to my dear Mama back home in Scotland, who was not happy with the way her life had turned out and her posture and demeanour spoke volumes. She and I were like the closest of sisters, totally in tune and we adored one another. My husband listened politely to the description of the dream and then the day took its course and I forgot all about it.

Later that day I spotted a Gideon's Bible in the hotel bedroom and picked it up. It fell open in my lap and as I read the print I was surprised to see it was a passage I knew.

'To everything there is a season
and a time to every purpose under the Heavens,
a time to be born and a time to die,
a time to plant and a time to reap...'

I didn't know my Bible and I was amazed it should open at a piece I knew so well. I recognized the words from an old 60's pop song called Turn, Turn, Turn by The Birds but I had no idea where to find them in the Bible. I made a mental note that it was Ecclesiastes, Chapter 3.

As we packed up our things that afternoon, ready to leave, my husband was called to the hotel reception for a phone message. There were no telephones in the bedrooms in those days. Some minutes later he returned, his face looking sombre and shaken. "There's a message from Colombo. A call from Scotland came through this morning. It's bad news, I'm afraid. Your Mother has died."

I looked hard into his face. I couldn't grasp what he was saying to me. 'What?' I whispered, 'Not possible?' I mouthed, shaking my head in disbelief. This couldn't be true, it must be a mistake. It couldn't be my Mother, she was so well, 64 years old last week, oh God it couldn't be.

The five-hour journey with potholes, bullock carts and stray cattle seemed to take forever. At last we were home and I could telephone Scotland. My stepfather answered and I knew the truth. Mummy had died in her sleep the night before, at approximately 8 p.m. She'd thought she had a touch of indigestion and had gone to bed early. Ian had gone to check later and had found her.

I was stunned. After a while I expressed my surprise that my Mother hadn't contacted me. We'd always promised one another that who ever died first, would try to get in touch with the other. There was a pause and then Gordon remembered my dream. I sat up and looked at him, eyes wide. Of course, that wonderful dream, how could I have forgotten. It seemed like a lifetime ago, but yes, I thought back, she was going on a journey, she was clearly jubilant, and she had a little weekend bag with her, a coat and a hat. Wasn't she brilliant! She had got through to me, the message was as clear as a bell. Then I remembered waking at around 1.30 a.m. and sorting out my bed for no reason at all. The time difference between the U.K. and Sri Lanka is five and a half hours. Mummy had died at approximately 8p.m. She had woken me at the time of her death.

I flew home for my Mother's funeral. She had always said that if anything happened to her I was not to return for her funeral, as they were pointless affairs. She had told me that she would be too busy investigating her new surroundings but from my point of view she was much mistaken.

On the morning of her funeral I was sitting at my dressing table, attempting to make the best of a grey and gaunt reflection. A frantic tweeting was going on outside my bedroom window but it didn't penetrate. The cheeping and twittering became a clamour. My mind was like a fog and it was only after about ten minutes that it dawned on me that there was some sort of disturbance and from where I was sitting, I looked out of the window.

I saw maybe eight to ten birds on the lawn, all looking in my direction about twenty feet away. What surprised me, even in my zombified state, was the fact that they all seemed to be in pairs, robins, thrushes, blackbirds, and sparrows. I only wish now that I'd registered more clearly what I was seeing.

I decided to check the lawn the following morning to see if this was a regular occurrence in October. I'd lived overseas for seventeen years and never returned in the autumn. I knew more about the bird life in the Far East than the dear little Sparrow in my Scottish garden.

Funnily enough, after I'd acknowledged the birds' presence, they stayed a few moments longer then quietly dispersed. Sure enough, the next morning, there was nothing to be seen, apart from a desultory blackbird worming methodically in the corner of the distant garden.

At the funeral, Reverend Gillespie spoke beautifully and to my surprise read the lovely piece I had found by chance, in the Gideon's Bible only days before, thousands of miles away in Sri Lanka. 'Coincidence.' I said to myself as I refused the tears. Mummy would not approve of tears, such self-indulgence.

He then went on to read another Lovely piece that I had heard before,

'Though I speak with tongues of men and of Angels
and have not charity,
I am as sounding brass, or a tinkling cymbal.
And though I have the gift of prophecy
and understand all mysteries and all knowledge
and though I have all faith, so that I could remove
mountains, and have not charity,
I am nothing.'

He read several verses. It was beautiful and so appropriate. My Mother had always been the most generous person.

As I drove home and turned into the gate, a squirrel sat in the driveway right in front of the car. He was sitting looking straight at me. I braked. He stared intently into my eyes. He stared and stared.. The engine was running but he was in no hurry. He was lovely but I had things to do, we couldn't sit here all day. Reluctantly I gently pressed the accelerator pedal. He didn't move. I pressed it again. On the third try I let the car roll forward a fraction and, still staring, he bounded four feet up the Chestnut tree to my immediate right, and stared again. Well, I had to smile. It was beginning to dawn on this bewildered and grief stricken lady that perhaps my Mama had more than a little something to do with all these goings on.

The next thing was to take my two young sons out of boarding school for a night in Perthshire. I had been given special permission. We stayed at the very grand Athol Palace Hotel, meant to be a real treat for us all. But, I was still in a fog-like state, behaving more like a robot. Still, I had the distinct feeling that the spirit world was guiding me, helping and nurturing me through this difficult time.

That evening, I noticed a Gideon's Bible by the bed. I picked it up absentmindedly as we waited for dinner and it fell open in my lap. It couldn't be, am I seeing things? The passage my eyes landed upon read,

'Though I speak with the tongues of men
and of Angels and have not charity,
I am become as sounding brass or a tinkling cymbal...'

I saw that it was Corinthian's, chapter thirteen. I hadn't known what it was or where to find it and here I was reading it.

At my Mother's funeral service, I had told myself that the reading of Ecclesiastes was merely a coincidence. Now here was Corinthian's and I knew that coincidence played no part. My darling Mama had been extremely busy on leaving this plane. She was doing her utmost to assure me, to get it through to me, that there was no such thing as death. 'You can't, you don't!' I could almost hear her sing.

And if you know that you don't die, can't die, then you surely are a most privileged person. This knowledge is my Mother's priceless gift to me.

What You Can Do

Offerings of Love

Uplifting music, singing, words and heartfelt wishes can soothe those who have died. They can be calmed by the perfume of flowers and candles as well as other aromas. Divine sounds and a lit candle also encourage beings of Light to gather round to help you and your beloved.

This is affirmed by different Spiritual traditions. In the East, incense as well as food is given ceremonially as a gift for and on behalf of the deceased. The smell of fresh food and fruit, incense and fragrant perfumes offered to those who have died are what food is to us. They are considered to be a powerful source of nourishment. Offerings are also given to the Guardians of the Afterlife, in gratitude for their help.

If your loved one had a favourite flower or perfume, offer this as a gift to their photograph. Also, during your sacred quiet times, play uplifting music for them. Dedicate all that you do with a prayer, asking for peace and healing for all concerned.

The Candle Ritual

Light a candle (preferably perfumed) each evening for your loved one. It may help you to write their name on a small piece of paper and place it under the candleholder with the intention of sending Light, as symbolised by the candle. It is important that you break through the barriers of your mind - a mind that tells you that they have gone and are unable to hear you or communicate with you. Trust your feelings and intuition rather than your mind. Feel gratitude and happiness for the connection you have had and still have.

Spend this sacred time of intimacy and healing in front of the candle. Close your eyes and relax your breathing. Imagine vividly your loved one beside you. It does not matter if you feel you have to pretend. Your imagination will help you to break through the barriers of your usual thought processes. Tell yourself that your beloved has not disappeared. Actually, now that they do not have a physical body separating you, their closeness can be greater than ever before. There is no real division between Heaven and earth! It is a matter of frequency, much the same as in tuning a radio. When you move from one radio station to the next, the station you leave behind does not cease to exist. It is only that you have moved to a different wavelength.

Be aware that your beloved will probably be more aware of you than you are of them. Your earthly, physical body gets in the way of subtle contact. The reality for them is that there is no such division. When you feel connected you will just know that you are. Speak aloud or mentally communicate what is happening. You can explain to your dear one that they have passed on and what this might mean for them. If you feel strong enough, talk to them about the forthcoming funeral and ask them to guide you as to their wishes. You may find it easier to write them a letter. When you have done so, place the letter in a sacred place in your home and keep a lit candle next to it.

During these quiet personal times, you can give positive encouragement to your dear one as well as communicating anything that has been left unsaid. If someone dies unexpectedly, there is no time to say, "I love you". You can now say these words and more, remembering that you have all the time in the world to say whatever needs to be said.

This sacred time can be helpful to one who has died and especially if they are not yet aware that they have passed, or if they are in a state of psychic shock. For the deceased, the circumstances of death can initially affect their consciousness and their adjustment to the loss of a physical body. If you feel your beloved may be in shock, repeatedly affirm what has happened to them with positive instructions and prayers to go to The Light.

Sacred Breathing

During the intensity of your loss, you may feel that you are not completely in your body or in reality. You may be in shock. To help you connect to your sense of self, to your body and your own life force, take a moment or two to read what follows. Let this exercise help you to identify with what is happening.

Identifying and relaxing into your present situation, will help you feel more grounded. The Now (the present moment) contains peace. Pain is normally connected to the past or the future - what we have experienced and what we fear we will experience. Your emotions and thoughts may change rapidly throughout the day, moment by moment. No, you are not going insane. On all levels of your being, you are adjusting, integrating and healing. This takes time and you have just begun.

Do you feel:

Confusion, disbelief, denial, numbness, shock, sadness, anger, despair, guilt, vulnerable, fear, relief, happiness, physical pain, nauseous, alone, isolated, lost, unable to go on, some other emotion, or do you feel nothing?

Stay with the feeling for a few moments and breathe deeply. Focus your awareness in your heart-area. Breathe in. Be aware that you are breathing in God (The Creator, The Light...). As you breathe out, be aware that you are breathing out you, who is One with God. As you complete an inhalation and exhalation, repeat internally "God and I are One." (5)

Place the palms of your hands at each side of your abdomen. After a few minutes place your hands over your abdomen and lovingly hold yourself like this for a short while.

Preparing for the Funeral

Take some moments to consider the structure and the implications of this crucial rite of passage for your loved one. What will be inspiring and healing for all concerned? Honour your loved ones requests. What prayers, poetry or music would be appropriate and which they liked? What flowers would your loved one like to choose? The more personal the ritual, the more soothing it will be for them.

If you are not directly involved in arranging these matters, what special prayers, music and ritual can you say and do, even in the privacy of your own home?

Prayers said at this time are particularly crucial. They will help to bring peace and clarity to your dear one and will help the Angelic beings from the spiritual realms to come close to them. No prayers go unheeded. And, they will help all involved to heal the pain and sorrow that is present. From the so-called primitive tribal societies of the world, to the seemingly most sophisticated, there is an awareness and belief that the deceased benefit from prayers. You can say these prayers personally or you can ask your local priest, minister, church, temple or any spiritual organization to say them for you.

Susannah tells us a wonderful and creative account of arranging a funeral.

A Painted Coffin

"What are you going to do about your funeral?" asked Ananda. I gulped at her blunt question. " I hadn't planned on going yet,' I thought but replied as candidly as I could to the dying woman before me, " As it happens I discussed this very subject some time ago with my eldest son and told him I wanted a painted coffin and balloons." Ananda chuckled in response and asked why? " Well it's like this," I said "I see my death as a celebration of a life and not something as morbid and sad, so as each balloon floats off up into the sky, there is my spirit flying free." We didn't talk about funerals again until the day before she died.

Ananda was suffering from a particularly voracious lymphoma, a cancer that consumed her body within 7 months. She was determined to live independently at home for as long as she could. Finally her body gave up.

I visited her the day after she had been admitted to St. Columba's Hospice in Edinburgh. It was a bright sunny afternoon in July. As I walked towards the hospice gardens I particularly noticed the peaceful atmosphere all around me. This was not a place of sadness but one of deep rest.

When I opened Ananda's door I saw her wraith like figure dressed in a white cotton nightgown walk painfully round her bed. But when she turned to look at me I shall never forget her eyes - they burned with a brightness and beauty that reflected the depth of her great soul. I was speechless and deeply moved.

"Susannah, I don't know whether to be buried or to have a woodland burial. I do Love the idea of a painted coffin by the way. Or maybe I should be cremated. In any case I won't be there will I?" She sighed wearily.

Early the next morning Ananda died very peacefully listening to her favourite music from Aurobindo's ashram, Pondicherry in India - A place that she had visited and loved and where she found inner contentment.

Ananda had no family left who could help, except for a cousin who was on holiday in Florida and unobtainable. Rosie who was also Ananda's friend and I met in Ananda's flat. We did not know each other well but this was no hindrance to us working together harmoniously. We became good friends. Rosie had found an excellent book in Ananda's small but comprehensive library called "The Natural Death Book." It was a fountain of information and practical help for those uninitiated in organizing funerals.

Whilst browsing through this book she discovered an undertaker in Edinburgh who arranged woodland burials. Over lunch we put our heads together about what to do. We both really liked the idea of a woodland burial and we felt Ananda would too. The rather utilitarian feel of a service in a crematorium was, we knew, something Ananda would not have liked.

The Edinburgh undertakers were very helpful and together we discussed the question of which coffin to choose including the option of cardboard. These came in three sizes, small, medium and large. There were no white cardboard coffins in stock - only a buff coloured one like a supermarket grocery box, but in its total ordinariness there lay its potential. We could paint it all the different colours of the rainbow and that is just what we did.

I felt what I was about to do would stay with me for the rest of my life. This was a direct and loving contribution to my friend, putting me in touch with her death in a very real and cathartic way. And she being an artist, I knew would have loved it all.

I painted the outside of the cardboard coffin. On the lid I designed a huge flower rising out of a plume of fire. Ananda was a rare flower indeed and she had been a very fiery lady! At her feet I painted an orange OM sign for she was a deep lover of God in the widest sense of the word. (OM being the primordial sound of the Universe and of course a symbol for her deep love of India).

I contacted a friend who was an Interfaith Minister as it struck me that she would be the right person for Ananda.

She had also travelled in India and so had a deep empathy from where Ananda was coming from spiritually.

It rained on the day of the funeral. So amidst the copper beech trees and umbrellas we circled around Ananda's grave and her colourful coffin. Kate conducted Ananda's funeral with great grace, putting together a ceremony that was absolutely right for her.

I felt Ananda's spirit fly free. We were all deeply moved. "Ananda, this has been a rare privilege. Thank you."

Notes

1. *Nadi leaves are believed to have been recorded thousands of years ago by the ancient Rishis. Several priests and astrologers in India claim access to them. They were often handed down through the generations of a family. The leaves are arranged according to an astrological filing system. When a seeker arrives, an astrological chart is drawn up for the moment of their arrival. A leaf matching the configuration should be available. This will give the spiritual seeker specific information about their past, present and future, and the actions of the past that are creating present problems. Nadi leaves were written to help spiritual seekers in future generations. I have known some people consult the Nadi to find that there is not a matching leaf.*

2. *It is believed by the Hindu and Buddhist traditions and some Shamanic ones, that if one's consciousness leaves the body through the Crown Chakra at the moment of death, one achieves Liberation and there is no need to reincarnate. That is, one does not need to return as an ego-personality bound by karma. Consciousness or the soul body energy can exit through any of the body's orifices. When the energy leaves through the Heart Chakra, it is believed that there is the opportunity for a human rebirth and not say, an animal or worse, however it will not be without attachment. I was told by the Nadi reader that I would leave my body at will through the Crown Chakra. Fortunately Sai Baba stopped me leaving through the Heart Chakra at that time.*

*If one has to be reborn, a human birth is said to be the best birth. To reincarnate as anything other than a human being is considered less helpful. There are specific instructions in **The Tibetan Book of the Dead** to help the one in the Bardo (the in-between Realms) to either avoid reincarnation altogether or, if this is not possible due to ignorance and karma, to at least be reincarnated in a human womb.*

'If you must take rebirth, or you intentionally wish to be reborn in order to pursue your spiritual path and be of benefit to others, you should not enter any but the human realm. It is only there that conditions are favourable for spiritual progress. If you are going to be born in a fortunate situation in the Human Realm, the teachings tell us, you will feel you are arriving at a sumptuous and beautiful house, or in a city, or among a crowd of people, or you will have a vision of couples making love.'

The Tibetan Book of Living and Dying - Sogyal Rinpoche

Belief in the Afterlife and Reincarnation is as varied as different religions, attitudes and people!

Here are some examples from less well-known world traditions.

The Balinese taught me that they conceive life on earth as one stage in the continuity of existence. The cycle begins at birth and is such a cherished event that the umbilical cord is preserved and kept for life. The birth is attended by the entire family as well as aided by their holy man who invokes spiritual powers to aid the delivery.
Death is a time when the soul is freed and finds rest as well as other possible experiences before being reborn.

The Celtic tradition (which is part of my own ancestry, being Scottish by birth) believes in the journey of the soul in the Spirit world and reincarnation as well as transmigration of the soul. A commonly held belief is of the spirit of the departed, entering stones or trees.

There is the famous tale of two ill-fated lovers, Deirdre and

Naoise. *After their tragic death, two pine trees grew from their graves, eventually re-uniting the Lovers as intertwined branches never to be parted.*

Trees and especially those that grow from a grave are still held as sacred by Celtic people.

3. Karma is the law of cause and effect. Even the most superficial relationships with others are caused through the connections and history we have had with them in previous lives. Some karmic connections are so powerful it takes many lifetimes to detach from them.

4. All spiritual teachings and religions tell us that there is life after death and most have specific prayers and rituals to help the one who is passing or who has passed. In the Christian Catholic tradition we have the Last Rights given before or just after death. The Buddhist and Hindu traditions have similar prayers. The teachings on death and the Afterlife may differ in different traditions, but the consensus is that death is not the end of the True Self.

*Some religions are very specific in detailing the stages of the experience of death and the Afterlife. The Tibetan Buddhist teachings contain **The Tibetan Book of the Dead**, which is an in-depth comprehensive account of what they believe happens at the time of death and in the Afterlife, on a physical, physiological, emotional and spiritual level.*

For example, these teachings tell us how, in death, after the last breath, the subtle energies of the body draw toward the heart area. They explain that the white subtle energy that sustains the masculine energy, received from one's father at the moment of conception and maintained in the crown of the head throughout one's life, drops toward the heart.

At this point, the now deceased is said to have a visual experience like moonlight. Then the red, feminine energy, received from one's mother at conception and maintained below the navel, rises toward the heart. The deceased one now has a visual experience of redness, like the sky at dawn or sunset. The masculine and feminine energies merge and the nearly deceased faints into unconsciousness, like passing into a deep, sleep. This is what Tibetan Buddhism states is death - a state from which there can be no recovery.

It is thought that the deceased one's consciousness at its most subtle level, can remain in the body for up to 3 days. The timing can be dependant on the circumstances of death. Sometimes, if death is accidental, the consciousness may leave instantly. But, at other times, especially after a peaceful death, the consciousness can remain for some days. Yogis and highly evolved beings can remain for many months even years and there are recorded cases of bodies, which do not decay. St Bernadette of Lourdes is one.

*5. This breathing exercise is inspired by the ancient breath meditation called So'ham from the ancient Indian Upanishad texts. **The Upanishads** are part of the Hindu scriptures. The So'ham vibration is considered to be inherent in us. It repeats itself continually, naturally, along with our breathing. Therefore, no matter what religion or faith you have, every time you complete a breath, you automatically chant the So'ham mantra.*

When you undertake to chant So'ham, you are merely making conscious what is already happening, even without you knowing. As you breathe, you inhale air and exhale air. Your breath comes in with the sound 'So' (God), and goes out with "Ham" (I - that is also God).

Between the inhalation and the exhalation, and between the exhalation and inhalation, there is a moment that is absolutely still and free of thoughts. This space is the space of your True Self, of the Divine, of God. You do not need to attain this. You already are That which is this space... It is merely a matter of understanding and knowing this.

forty-nine days

Grief and Surrender

Chapter 2

Reflections

Days Four to Nine

'O Arjuna! You are grieving because these kings
and princes who are related to you are about to meet
their death at your hands. You talk glibly of Dharma.
But remember, the wise do not grieve either for the living or
the dead. Shall I tell you why? Well, you are grieving over
the body which alone decays on death. Did you grieve when
the body underwent many changes hitherto?
The child disappeared in the boy, the boy disappeared
in the youth, the youth became lost in the middle-aged
man, the middle-aged man was lost in the aged old man
and the old man is lost in death.
You never wept for the changes that affected the body so long.
Why then weep for this one change?
Have you, today, the body you had when you were a boy?'

Sri Sathya Sai Baba

In the famous spiritual epic of the **Bhagavad Gita**, (6) Krishna says the above evocative words to Arjuna, who is about to go into battle against his kith and kin. Death is not what we think - the body alone decays on death - the legendary words say. Death is not something to be forgotten until she strikes. Death is to be remembered as every cell, every age within us dies. Death is to be welcomed as it offers new life and a greater meaning to our short existence here.

★ ★ ★

Your loved one has left the body for more than three days. A Divine revolution is taking place within them, in you, which affects all concerned. Meet the transformation that is happening with as much openness as possible. Life is indefinite. There is no certainty in life or in death. Courage is needed to trust the Unknown. It takes grit to meet the challenge of uncertainty with trust and acceptance. There is really no choice here. Trying to run and hide behind comforting delusions or addictions is no escape.

★ ★ ★

Cigarettes, comfort food, alcohol, repetitive negative patterns of behaviour, will only delay your progress, perhaps even for lifetimes. Fear and doubt will split you from your path and destroy you. Vacillation will get you nowhere and will delay the process that must take place on every level of your being. That is, the realisation of what this death really is and its meaning in your life. You cannot do this with the ego in control. True mutiny of the ego requires your conscious effort. This positive step cannot happen without you! Vigilance is essential. Remember to trust. Have faith.

★ ★ ★

'Death is not an end, but a new beginning.
Under the stress of conflicting passions and earthly desires,
biological cravings and love of pleasure and power,
is hidden an eternal stream of pure consciousness
which is not affected by the law of cause and effect
and which is ever tranquil bliss and freedom,
real Love and truth.
This is the real Self of man.'

Hari Prasad Shastri

★ ★ ★

Can you make the commitment to surrender yourself, your grief and your uncertainty, by taking the simple decision to hand over the process of your deep healing and that of your dear one, to a Higher Power. Whether you believe that this Higher Power is within you or external to you is irrelevant. Have faith in surrendering and in the awareness that you are involved in a process that has its own timing. Do not compare. Everyone has their own time of healing. You are unique. Remember that at this time, at anytime, you do not know what will be the stages of your journey and how they will unfold.

There will be a great pulling and pushing going on within you. Every part of you is in shock and trauma. Your body, organs, central nervous system, mind as well as your subtle bodies, your energy field are battling with fear, frustration, panic and grief. It will be at times overwhelming. In such a confused state, your mind cannot function rationally. Let go trying to do or understand. Visualise yourself being held in Divine hands of Love. Imagine you are curling into the lap of God like a very tiny child. Breathe. Hand yourself over.

★ ★ ★

As you lie down on the hand of God, relinquish your need to know what is right. Let go of your need to be in control. You now have the opportunity to go past the limitations and naivety of the human condition, to find That which is normally hidden by the illusion of worldly things, routines and comforts. Letting go and surrendering is the elevated road to Peace. Trying to do it all by yourself is the road to pain.

★ ★ ★

'When you have surrendered yourself completely to God and become God's child, you don't have to tell God what you want. He will give even more than you have asked for. But it is only by Love that He is your dearest.'

Sri Sathya Sai Baba

★ ★ ★

Since death, your loved one may have experienced themselves as though in a dream. At this time, they may awake and have some anxiety. You too might feel as though you have been anaesthetized. When the numbness wears off, your pain may be intense, as further awareness and recognition of what has happened occurs. You may suffer bombardment from a myriad of overwhelming and conflicting feelings and emotions. As your beloved is required to hold fast to the idea of A Higher Power, to God, in whichever way is most acceptable, so too are you.

* * *

Buddha, Allah, Jesus, The Great Mother, The Higher Self, The Light. It does not matter in which form or from which creed you choose. What matters, is that you connect and stay connected to Love. Your beloved is going through the Bardo Realm, (7) the in-between worlds. And in a different dimension, so are you. Your bond and desire for connection with Truth and Love will take you through. Keep mourning. Do not put on a brave face unless you really have to. Do not enter denial.

* * *

'Blessed are those who mourn,
for they shall be comforted.'

Matthew

* * *

To help this critical shift, talk to your dear one. Read this book aloud to them and any other book that is about death and God. Help to clear any confusion in their mind. Talk to them about their death and their Afterlife. Tell them that there is no going back for the body has died.

★ ★ ★

'Death is part of our lives.
Whether we like it or not, it is bound to happen.
Instead of avoiding thinking about it,
it is better to understand its meaning.
We all have the same body, the same human flesh
and therefore we will all die...
If from the beginning your attitude is
"Yes, death is part of our lives,
then it may be easier to face.'

His Holiness the XIV Dalai Lama

★ ★ ★

Advise your beloved to stay focussed on images of the Divine. Describe a Mandala of Light, (8) in which at the very centre there is the manifestation of their personal idea of God, encircled by a host of angelic beings and the great Masters of Truth.

Tell them to visualise this image and stay focussed with all possible strength remaining fixed on the dazzling luminous ray that emanates from the heart-centre of the Mandala. Help your beloved to not be distracted or to stray elsewhere where the light is more subtle or diffused. You can imagine the same visualisation in your own way, praying fervently that you are never again distracted from the light of Love and Truth and that you may vigilantly follow the Path of Truth until you reach Home. (9)

★ ★ ★

'During the first weeks of the Bardo,
we have the impression that we are a man or woman,
just as in our previous life.
We do not realize that we are dead.
We return home to meet our family and loved ones.
We try to talk to them, to touch them on the shoulder.
But they do not reply, or even show
they are aware that we are there.
As hard as we try, nothing can make them notice us...'

Sogyal Rinpoche

★ ★ ★

With the awareness of their death your loved one may experience grief at leaving their life behind. Also, it is likely that they will be aware of your grief. The time is highly sensitive. Your beloved is in a highly sensitive state. You are in a highly sensitive state. As Sogyal Rinpoche writes, your loved one may try to talk to you or touch you but it is not possible. This is distressing. In Bardo of Becoming, my novel of a journey after death, Paul wakes up in the in-between world as though from a long dream. He finds himself by his wife's side. He does not realise that he is dead or that she cannot see him.

"Thank God, I've woken up... I'm here, Maria... I'm here... Thank God..."

But she was not smiling at him or teasing him. She did not even look at him. She seemed oblivious to his presence. She looked lost and sad and she was crying. Her eyes were red and swollen and her pale bone-china skin was blotchy. She looked like she had been crying for days, weeks... "God," he said in an automatic plea for help, "she looks so sad." He felt distraught to see her like this. What had happened to make her so sad, so tired, so beaten and weary looking? She looked like she had lost the whole world.

"Maria, Darling - Beloved, I am here. Don't cry." He tried to place his arms around her to comfort her but they made no contact with any part of her and fell down as though to the ground as they passed right through her. It was as if he had invisible arms, as though his arms did not exist. She moved away from him and lay down on the bed on her side, in a foetal position with her legs curled up to her belly, turning her face away from him. She acted as though she did not see him. She behaved as though she could not even hear him. She treated him like he was dead.

"Maria, look at me...look at me...I'm here." There was no response from the huddled figure. Panic stirred within him and waved through his body and as it became more like choppier and choppier energy swells passing through him, he felt nauseous. He felt that he wanted to be sick. He retched and then could not stop. But there was nothing in his stomach to come out...

★ ★ ★

Help your dear one to not have the same experience as Paul. Your Love is like an anchor. It will save your beloved from drowning in the sea of despair and illusion. Talk to them and explain to them how they have died and how much you Love them. Be positive and strong for their sake. Tell your loved one that although you cannot hold one another with your bodies and arms you can embrace each others hearts.

In this way you can bring home to your loved one that they are dead. Connecting, reaching out, communicating about what has happened will help them let go and realise that there is no going back. They will avoid too what some deceased encounter, as written in a passage of the **Garuda Purana**:

> 'Reaching the Death Realm
> he remains there for a little period,
> then returns to the Men's realm,
> after getting permission from Yamaraja.
> As he reaches the mortal world,
> he tries to re-enter his old body...
> he doesn't succeed.'

* * *

Handle your loved ones belongings respectfully. Try to make sure that others do the same. Imagine how you would feel to be dead, to see your possessions yet be unable to touch them or use them? How would you feel to see people sifting through personal items that mean so much to you, assessing them, desiring them, or even fighting over them? Connect with your beloved in your heart and ask them to guide you as to what they wish you to do with their belongings. The Angels and Beings of Light who are helping your beloved will also help to inspire you about your dear one's wishes.

* * *

As well as feeling that they are not being heard and cannot be held by their loved ones, your loved one is unable to assuage their hunger or thirst in the same way as before. And yet the desire to do so may be there. Harmonious music and sounds, beautiful fragrances offered in Love to them are food for the soul, comforting as a soothing balm. It is the subtle body that now needs fed. The greatest nourishment the subtle body can receive is Love. The real hunger is hunger for God's Love. Compassion will make your loved one feel fully nourished.

* * *

Pray to all the Beings of Light, the Angel Realms, the Guardians, to help soothe and ease your dear one from their plight. Prayer is healing and transformational, as well as a plea to the Divine. Whenever you can, pray aloud. If your surroundings do not allow external prayer, pray silently, internally.

* * *

Danger comes from clinging to attachment, desiring, fearing, and resisting change. In holding on to these, your loved will long for a comfort that cannot be met. If you too hold on in this way, you will find no real relief to your suffering. Our cravings bring restlessness and grief. Try to remain open, strong and flexible. Let go of longings, other than a longing for God.

Sathya Sai Baba has given the example of a large strong tree on which thousands of birds are resting. Their droppings on the ground make the tree unusable. How do we drive the birds away? When you shout the name of God and clap your hands, they will fly away.

The birds are like our desires. They live in us and pollute our heart. To get rid of them, you have to shout the name of God with intent and they will fly away.

★ ★ ★

Feel rooted in your own self like a strong oak. Bend like a willow. Cling to God like a vine and never let go.

★ ★ ★

When you remember your loved one, visualize them as flawless, filled with light, happiness and Love. This is their true nature. To think of them in such a way, will help them to think well of themselves. It will remind them that this is their true nature. It will remind both of you to stay positive and happy. When you think of your beloved at any time, in prayer, or sitting quietly in communion with them, remember their face at its most beautiful, when their smile was at its most radiant.

Lesley relates the following touching account.

The Radiant Smile

I am reminded of my mother in law who died following a difficult time with a form of dementia. Often when we visited her she would not recognise us. I must say that it frightened me a little because she was not the woman I remembered and loved. She had been so cheerful, generous and loving to everyone, particularly her family. It was a cruel blow to see her so anxious and haunted in her last days.

I can still recall the last time I saw her. She was in hospital being awkward and angry with everyone who was trying to help her - the nurses, my husband and I. My husband had to leave the room to take a phone call. I remained, and as I watched this frail old lady, I saw the most angelic, blissful smile lighten and brighten her face. The years and the cares melted away. I was the only witness.

She died two days later. I went to see her body. It was the first dead body I had ever seen. Although a nerve-wracking experience, I was so pleased I had seen her. As I looked at her body, I knew that although it looked peaceful, it was just a shell. The real May was not there anymore. She was within that radiant and loving smile I had been privileged to witness before she died. The memory still links me to all the wonderful joy that was part of her human life and which I now look for in everyone I meet, whatever trials they are passing through.

★ ★ ★

Many people give themselves a hard time when someone close to them dies. They are filled with regret and remorse. They remember their last conversation and wish it had been different. Or, if they were not present at the time of death, they find it difficult to forgive themselves.

When I nursed patients who were dying, I observed many times, how the dying one would wait until their nearest and dearest left the room before taking their last breath. Often, they would wait by the dying one's bedside for many hours unwilling to leave in case their loved one needed them. They would go quickly for a cup of tea or a bite to eat, only to find on returning that their loved one had died in the interim.

Believe that everything is perfect in its own way. From a wider, Divine view, it is good to die when a loved one is not present. It helps the soul fly more freely from the body.

If there are things you would rather not have said or done, be kind with yourself. It is the nature of life that we make mistakes and that we do not always know what is good for us at any given time. Making mistakes, suffering through them, rectifying them if possible, changing yourself because of them, is intrinsic to your growing spiritual maturity. This is the way we learn. Learn to Love yourself as God Loves you - unconditionally and with compassion. You can only do your best. This is enough to receive God's loving Grace.

★ ★ ★

Remind yourself that we can never know what is good for others. This is because we have a limited mind-view. Only God has the wider view. We cannot see the bigger picture in any situation. Only God does. For example, when we hear of the death of a child, we automatically feel sadness that such a youngster is cut from life. But, from God's point of view the child may be a very old and wise soul. Perhaps, the few years in this life was all that was needed to journey home. (9)

All we can do is offer our confusion and lack of wisdom to The Source of All-knowing and allow what is perfect to unfold. This is what humility really is - openness. And when we are truly humble, truly open, anything can happen. Even miracles.

* * *

'… Can sorrow end?
It can only come to an end
when you understand yourself,
which is actually 'what is'.
Then you understand why you have sorrow,
whether that sorrow is self-pity,
or the fear of being alone,
or the emptiness of your own life,
or the sorrow that comes about
when you depend on another.
And all this is part of our living.'

J Krishnamurti

Do not isolate yourself from help. Make a point of being with those who comfort and Love you. Do what is easy, simple and good. If there are difficulties, obstacles, tensions, draw back and rest. Go with the flow and don't push where there is a wall. This will allow you to see God do God's work for you in the kindest and most loving way.

* * *

In this time of hardship, the fruits of your suffering are a deeper maturity and openness of heart. Remember this. Stay open, remain loving, embrace all by praying,

Let my healing and understanding be Thy will and not my will and for the good of all concerned.

* * *

At this time, it is likely that your dear one is highly telepathic and clairvoyant. Now use these days of heightened communication as positively as possible. Know that you will be heard. Do not doubt this and continue to do your utmost in helping your loved one realise the wonderful possibilities available to them. Talk to them of their new life, of freedom, of God, of Love in its highest level. Encourage happiness, surrender, letting go and the need to move on... from the form and the life they have been attached to. It is gone forever and there is no coming back. Sing devotional songs and prayers. Help lighten the path ahead for your loved one. Help lighten the path for your little vulnerable self.

* * *

Liken what is happening to them to a deep state of meditation. When we meditate our consciousness expands as we withdraw from the senses. We initiate the mind into the purest sense of "I." Here, there is the revelation of the Self. Here, we cease to be a separate ego-personality. Here, we are One with Love and Love is what we manifest.

* * *

The deceased have every right to be happy. They are free of the limitations of a physical body, perhaps even a very painful one. Those who have died are free from the limitations of the physical senses and the constrictions they bring. But, if there is strong dependency between the one left behind and the one moving on, this creates sadness and restricts development. In the Afterworld attachment hampers the spiritually journey to finer, more subtle realms and states of consciousness. Be aware of this in all your communications and prayers with your beloved.

* * *

Before she died, the present Dalai Lama's mother, Diki Tsering, poignantly recalled how the Tibetan people of her generation believed that if one wept too much when someone died, the dead would not find their final destination.

'It was said that parent's tears would be like hail on a dead child's face. So I always controlled myself when my children died, no matter how intense my suffering, and I told my husband not to cry, for this reason.'

Diki Tsering, known as Gyayum Chenmo, Great Mother, gave birth to sixteen children. Only seven survived past infancy.

★ ★ ★

'Lay not up for yourselves treasures upon earth,
where moth and rust doth corrupt,
and where thieves break through and steal:
But lay up for yourselves treasures in Heaven,
where neither moth nor rust doth corrupt,
and where thieves do not break through nor steal.'

Jesus

★ ★ ★

While in the body, you have the opportunity to realise the crippling effects of attachment and dependency. You will be much more prepared when it is your time to pass from this world if you identify what these are and free yourself from them now. As far as possible, remain positive when you think of your loved one.

Keep your mind elevated. Be confident. When you think of your loved one believe that they have gone to a better place. Do not be sad for them. Cultivate a feeling of happiness for them. Be aware that your grief is to do with you and your own feelings of loss. Endeavour to care more for your loved one than for yourself.

The kinds of feelings you have about your loss reveal older, deeper emotions within you, which obscure your own birthright of happiness. What better gift can you give one another in this earthly separation than the gift of your blossoming freedoms? There is no hurry. It will all take time. One cannot wipe out lifetimes of patterns and ways of being in days, weeks or even months. But, with wisdom, intention and motivation you will have Divine support and grace to achieve your wish. All beings must prepare for death, even those who are Realised and have found freedom from suffering in this life.

★ ★ ★

The Buddha predicted that He would pass away in three months time on the full moon of May. He had been teaching for nearly half a century. Ananda, the Buddha's closest companion and disciple was yet to realize Enlightenment. He begged the Buddha to remain in his body as he could not bear to be alone without Him.

With great compassion, Buddha gently reminded him that it is in the nature of all forms to pass away and to leave all that is near and dear. He explained how everything brought into being contains within itself the inherent predisposition for dissolution. One of the last directives the Buddha gave was:

'Hold fast to the Truth and the Discipline as a lamp.
Seek deliverance alone in the Truth. Strive on with diligence. Free yourself from the tangled net of sorrow and dissatisfaction. Look not for assistance to anyone besides yourself. In regard to the body and the mind, let one be mindful and overcome the greed, which arises from the

body's craving, which arises from craving for sensations, which arises from craving due to ideas, reasons and emotions. If one is mindful, seekers of Truth shall surely reach the top-most pinnacle of Emancipation. But they must be willing to learn.'

* * *

Near the time of Buddha's death, many of the town and village folk of Kusinara gathered around him as he lay on a couch between two Sal trees. The Buddha turned to Ananda, "You wonder who will lead the Sangha. Whatever Dhamma (Truth) and Vinaya (discipline) has been taught by me, that will be your teacher when I am gone." He asked the monks if they had any doubts. They were silent. "Subject to change are all compounded things. Strive on with diligence!" These were the last words of the Buddha.

But the Buddha has never died. His Love and words of wisdom have continued for more than two thousand years to help people find Truth and freedom as he did.

* * *

Use your grief as a means to reflect on what many of the great sages and saints have told us throughout the ages, that life is indeed a preparation for death. Use this time of mourning to go even deeper into what life and death really mean to you. Do not hurry. There is no race and there is no finishing line. Grieving has its own time and its duration will be as individual and unique as your own heart.

In truth, no one can really get over the loss of someone very near and dear. Your souls were and are inextricably bound to one another. Now that they are physically gone, your life will never be the same again. This is a fact. You will adjust to this new life. You will find happiness in a different way, with a different kind of understanding.

Continue with the flow of your mourning - accept it. The river of your grief will lead you to the ocean of God's Love and intention for you. You will heal and accept this new life more quickly if you continue to trust that there is no end to Love - no final parting for you or anyone. There can be no final parting because the two is a temporary illusion. There is only one Eternal Self.

★ ★ ★

Love-Gratitude

The agony is so great…
And yet I will stand it.
Had I not loved so very much
I would not hurt so much.
But goodness knows I would not
want to diminish that precious Love
by one fraction of an ounce.
I will hurt,
and I will be grateful to the hurt
for it bares witness to
the depth of our meanings,
and for that I will be
eternally grateful.

Elisabeth Kuber-Ross

There is no need to fear the sight or sound of someone who has passed from this world. Even someone you love. Yes, it can be unnerving, especially if one is not used to it. But remember that you are both spirits. The only difference between you is that one has a physical body and one has a subtle body. As a child, Lesley, who wrote earlier of her mother-in-law's smile had the experience of seeing the subtle body of her grandmother. Initially, it was a quite frightening experience for her but one from which she eventually learned something very wonderful.

We Are All Living Spirits

I don't see my grandmother from the spirit world now, but I did before, when I was younger. Her words will never leave me. "Take my arm. Don't be afraid! They won't harm you, nothing can - you are a living spirit. "Dear Nanny. Bless her. I wasn't ready to listen to her at the time. It has taken over 35 years to begin to understand her simple message to me.

Nanny was my father's mother and she died when I was in my mid-teens. She lived with us, and my sister Alison and I must have been a great trial for her as we were often naughty and thoughtless. She had been the stereotypical late Victorian/Edwardian woman and she seemed really out of touch with what teenagers in the late 1960s were all about.

She had received treatment for glaucoma and was partially sighted. Nanny frequently wore a fox-fur trim and carried a white stick. Her laugh always sounded like a little cough at first. One night, Alison had an argument with her and stormed out of her room.

The next morning we found Nanny in a coma. She died shortly afterwards. Alison was distraught that she and Nanny had parted in anger and I was frightened. I couldn't go into her room. I was too scared to see a dead person. I was even scared to walk close to the door of her room.

I plucked up courage to watch her coffin be carried out of our house. My Dad was one of the pall-bearers. I didn't go to the funeral. I was not allowed to. My parents tried to spare my sister and I from further distress.

I don't remember how long it was after these events, when I first became aware of Nanny's presence. I hadn't been able to sleep and I could feel her in my bedroom. I did not believe she was there. I asked her, "If you are really there Nanny, prove it to me!" As the words came out of my mouth, a picture slid of the wall and crashed to the floor.

The second occasion, I actually saw Nanny. I was in a house full of friends and I felt a cold sweat come over me. I went out to wash my hands. I felt frightened and rushed back to join my friends. I could hear Nanny's white stick before I saw her. She appeared in the doorway, wearing her coat and fox-fur collar and carrying her white stick. I felt so scared, I sat rooted to my chair. I didn't see her move, but suddenly I saw her stand behind a friend seated on the other side of the room. Nanny spoke to me and told me not to be afraid. She said strange things were about to happen to me and that she would be with me. She then disappeared.

No one else saw her, but a couple of the others said that they had felt very cold. "Don't be afraid." Nanny said. I was terrified. I wasn't ready for this. Seeing ghosts isn't something that nice, normal teenage girls do. And besides, this was my grandmother, and she looked just as I remembered her in life, complete with the white tapping stick.

Nanny was right. Strange things did happen to me. I became very psychically open and could see all manner of things, which other people did not see. I continued to see Nanny and gradually I came to trust her as I became more used to seeing her in this way.

I had visions too during those years rather like visual meditations. Here is part of something I wrote at the time about one of them.

"Walking through a garden I saw a small side path. "Don't go down there!" An inner friend said.

"Why not?" I replied.

"Come on! I'll help you."

The path led on into a labyrinth. "What is this? Where does it lead?" I asked.

"This is the path of your life. Now you've left them and come with me, I will help but you must decide the route to the end." He told me.

My friend had to leave at a junction. Three roads met mine. Three people were waiting. My friend explained, "If you take the path with your mother as guide, you will end up nowhere. If you go with a friend he will lead you to more friends. If you let your dead grandmother lead the way, you will gain everything but lose much."

I thanked him and went with my grandmother. "Take my arm. Don't be afraid!" she said to me. " They won't harm you, nothing can - you are a living spirit."

Thank you Nanny for being there for me when life was not easy. I believe we are all living spirits. This is the most profound simple truth Nanny taught me.

★ ★ ★

'You are not the body,
a bundle of flesh, blood and bones.
Neither are you the unmanifested desires,
nor the manifested mind.
You are also not the infatuating delusion
that thwarts your liberation.
But you are the Eternal Paramatman,
if only you recognize your innate power.
The body, the senses
the mind and the intellect
are only the vestures put on by man.
Only when we understand the nature and significance
of these adjuncts,
can we make proper use of them.'

Sri Sathya Sai Baba

★ ★ ★

Dear One,
time feels so strange.
Sometimes our time together
seems like years
and at other times,
it is as though we had just met
when you left.

The time we had together
feels like just a moment
in the face of eternity

But I wonder, where were you
before we met
and where are you now?
Are you really gone from me?
Or, are you still with me
on another plane I can't see?

Perhaps somewhere we are dancing,
happily sharing our hearts.
Maybe it is only here,
where I think I am now,
that we are apart.

Some days, I find that
I cannot believe you are dead.
Can life ever accept death?
And yet I knew as I looked
at your beautiful closed eye-lids
that you had left me.

One day it will be my turn
to venture into the unknown -
to fly towards the Uncreated Light
from where we first came
and to which you have returned.

I will meet you there my dear,
In The Light,
that has no beginning
and no end.
Where there is
no such thing as pain.

* * *

Amanda and Graeme
A Love That Could Not Die

Amanda's husband Graeme, died in 1998 leaving her with
two children. Her story of the events following Graeme's
death is evocative, poignant and painful. Yet it is a story of
hope, promise and of the power of undying Love. Amanda
writes,

I had known Graeme since I was twelve years old. As
soon as I met him I felt I had known him before and bizarrely,
I knew that he would always be in my life. We were close
friends at the age of fourteen and best friends by the age of
sixteen. At the age of nineteen, Graeme was diagnosed with
leukaemia. This was a total shock for all who knew him as he
had never been ill and was full of life.

Later, I met Graeme by chance shortly after leaving a violent and abusive relationship. He was my rock. We started a relationship in June, became engaged in August, married in November and I was pregnant by December! We were both twenty-three years old.

Our first son was born in September 1993 and a year later Graeme had a bone marrow transplant. It was an initial success and although he had been to Hell and back, our future had hope. Devastatingly, eleven months later the leukaemia returned. Our second son was born in 1996.

Graeme appeared healthy and our outlook was still hopeful. In December 1997 we were told that Graeme's leukaemia had progressed and they gave him three months to live. I persuaded him to go to a well known NFSH healer in Scotland. I believe, and his consultant believed that these healing treatments gave him an extra year of life.

While Graeme was on business on 27th July 1998 (his twenty-ninth birthday) he suffered a brain haemorrhage. He survived but never worked again and for the last six months of his life I nursed him at home with immense Love.

Graeme was dying in his mother's arms and mine on Wednesday 30th Dec 1998 at 12.30pm. As he took his last breath I gave him to his mum. It seemed only right that as she had brought him into this world, she should hold him when he left it. I can truthfully say I never once in all my married life thought that this amazing and wonderful person would die. I was in complete and utter denial. When I married my husband he was seventeen and a half stone and when he died, he barely weighed nine and a half stone.

In the moments after Graeme died, I felt as though everything was surreal. I sat by his body for about forty minutes before leaving to tell those who loved him that we had lost him. I thought that if I told people that he had gone, I perhaps could start to believe it myself. When I stood up and tried to walk, it felt as though my shoes had been placed in concrete, because I could hardly lift my feet.

When I returned home I told our sons that their Daddy had gone to Heaven to get magic medicine to make him better. My eldest son asked, did that mean he was dead and not returning. I said yes and the look on his face will stay with me for the rest of my life.

It was Christmas time and we had a Christmas tree. In despair, I lunged at the eight foot tree attacking and kicking it. This would become a regular occurrence, once the children had gone to bed, however it was my kitchen cupboards that I would kick. I would have a drink of wine, cry until I ached then I would kick the doors until they came off their hinges. I replaced my kitchen six months later. I had to. There was not one unscathed cupboard door. My father panicked when he saw the violence. He wanted a Doctor to prescribe drugs for me but I told him I could cope.

More than five hundred people came to the funeral and we collected well over £2,500 for charity. Throughout the day I kept wishing Graeme could be there. I knew he would have loved to meet everyone. I felt very alone.

I had two small children to take care of and in the months to follow, I sometimes resented their needs. But I never once neglected them. Life for them continued more or less as before - only without their father. I did not have time to feel sorry for myself. I was far too busy looking after my family and supporting friends. Unbeknown to them I was drinking far too much. I sobbed through each night for six months while my children slept. For six to eight months after Graeme's death, I regularly phoned his work number to tell him something. I would hear the voice of his replacement answer and feel foolish and embarrassed. Each time was like a hard slap across my face.

Something happened about three to four weeks after Graeme's death. I physically ached to hold Graeme and I worried about who was looking after him in the spirit world. They did not know what he liked or needed, I thought. He needed me; I was the only one who could care for him. He needed me and I needed him.

I bathed and put my sons to bed and began the nightly ritual of drinking and crying. The more I drank, the more I wanted to see Graeme. After two bottles of wine I decided that I would join him. I kissed my sons as they slept, went downstairs and collected a bottle of whisky, two hundred Paracetamols, and boxes of Diamorphin (heroin that had been Graeme's painkillers while he was dying). I probably had enough drugs and alcohol to kill five people.

I honestly believed that I had to be with Graeme. I ached for his smell, the feel of his skin, the sound of his voice, the warmth of his smile and the sparkle of his eyes. I started with the Paracetamol. I had taken about ten to fifteen tablets washed down with whisky, when there was an almighty thud from upstairs. I ran to find that my eldest son had fallen out of bed. I put him back in bed and kissed him. I looked at my two wonderful sons and I realised that I could not make them orphans. They had lost a Father. It was selfish of me to take their Mother away from them as well. I was absolutely devastated. I knew that it would be a lifetime before I could be re-united with Graeme. (I was told many years later by a spiritual medium who did not know the story, that my husband had deliberately pushed our son out of the bed).

I went downstairs and put the drugs outside the back door. I went to bed weeping. I felt gutted that I could not be with my husband. I sensed the atmosphere in the room change dramatically. Suddenly from the wardrobe at the bottom of my bed a very familiar silhouette appeared and started walking towards me. I was not afraid. It was Graeme.

I felt the bed actually bend as he sat down beside me. I felt myself being lifted up into his arms. For a brief moment there was total bliss. I thought I was dying and he was here to collect me. Graeme held me in his arms and I felt the softness of his skin. He had gained back his weight. He was like the old Graeme. As he held me in his arms he gently rubbed both my arms at the same time. This was something we did throughout our time together when we had a bad report from the hospital about his health. No words could comfort him when the news was distressing. We would rub each others arms as a way of comfort, knowing full well that no promises could be made. But, that no matter what, we would always be there for each other.

Graeme gently let me go, got up and walked back towards the wardrobe. In his way he was telling me that I had our boys to look after, but that he would always be by our side.

Looking back almost seven years to that visit, there is not a day that goes by when I don't think of Graeme. It has been difficult to forge a new life for my sons and myself but I have tried. I know Graeme lives on, and very occasionally when life has been cruel to me I have felt his presence extremely close to me.

I know our Love for each other is as strong if not stronger than when Graeme was alive. My family minister said very wise words to me when Graeme died. "Your Love does not die when your loved one dies, it continues because Love is eternal." Our Love is eternal.

What You Can Do

Prayers After the Funeral

Prayers do not end at the Funeral Service. You can continue with formal or more personal prayers for your loved one for as long as you wish to. Prayer works. The effect of prayer can be likened to giving someone who has an economy plane ticket, a first-class upgrade. Prayers have tremendous flying power!

Not only that, but with the power of prayer, the destination too can change. Metaphorically, your dear one, living in a location like London, may have the resources to go to Europe. But, with the right help, they can do a world tour. This is the power of prayer. Prayers offer Divine support and their nature is miraculous.

Furthermore if your loved one is in pain, if they are suffering from the trauma of having died and leaving those they Love behind, or having difficulty adjusting to the different states of Consciousness in which they find themselves, prayers are a healing, soothing balm.

Prayers are an expression of Love, and of compassionate care asking the Divine to take over the great responsibility of the soul, our loved one's and our own. They vibrate into the Cosmos like exquisite music, heralding the Angels and Guardians to gather around and help in whatever way possible.

Different traditions have their own rituals and ways to honour and aid the deceased. The Synagogues remember the dead on a Friday evening. Catholics celebrate Holy Mass on behalf of someone who has died to help absolve their sins and enable the soul to progress to Heaven. Hindus do many rituals. One, is placing a photograph of the deceased one on a home-made altar. Daily prayers and other offerings, like beautiful scented flowers are given in remembrance.

Throughout the ages, mankind has attempted to help the deceased as it makes its initial journey into the Great Mystery of the Afterlife. Similarly, from the times of recorded history, we know that mourners from uniquely different cultures and traditions from all over the world have remembered and honoured the passing of a loved one.

In Tibetan Buddhism, prayers are said every seven days on the weekly anniversary of the death. These prayers are formally practised for forty-nine days as it is believed that the astral/mental body re-experiences its death on the seventh-day anniversary of the actual passing. (10)

You do not have to be a Tibetan Buddhist to do the seven-week ritual of offering and remembering. If your heart desires it, do the weekly ritual of prayers in your own special way. You may decide to have the prayers read by a religious or spiritual celebrant, arrange to say them with a group of friends or quietly by yourself.

Tibetan Buddhists have a special way of working out the timings of prayers. If your loved one died on a Saturday before noon, the seven-day prayer anniversary would be on the following Friday and thereafter every Friday for at least seven weeks. If the timing of the death was after noon, the anniversary would fall on the Saturday.

You do not have to follow this guideline, although it makes sense to use tried and tested methods that are considered beneficial. What is important here is your intention and sincerity. Without Love, any offering is but an empty, hollow vacuum.

Offerings

Not only prayers, but offerings of alms to the poor, to Spiritual Masters, holy places, churches, temples, monasteries, can be given on behalf of and for the benefit of your loved one. Offerings like these work in the same way as prayers. They are prayers in action. If you offer prayers in action, make an initial dedication on behalf of your loved one. This directs the positive vibrations and energies that result from the offering. As positive effects happen over a period of time, (and there is no doubt that this will happen), Divine support will be lodged in your beloved's spiritual bank account for use whenever needed.

I recently looked after an elderly American man in India during the last few months of his life. He was a devotee of Sai Baba and had lived in India for many years. One of his last wishes was to offer his expensive US electric sewing machine to a poor Tibetan family, so that they may have a better existence. Michael was not a Buddhist but he had a fondness for Tibetan people, their culture and religious philosophy.

Shortly after he died, two friends and I travelled from Bangalore to a Tibetan Settlement in Karnataka some 12 hours drive away, to carry out Michael's wishes. One of the regional Tibetan Buddhist monasteries I have a close connection with, suggested an underprivileged family to whom the sewing machine could be given. The family included a young mother who had a gift for tailoring.

They were very poor but greeted us with loving and generous hospitality. The elderly mother of the house showed us her altar and her daily prayer offerings to the Tibetan Buddhist Deities. She told us that she would pray every day for Michael in thanks for his generosity. Her offer to say daily prayers for Michael was indeed beautiful and as the family prospers, a little bit of Michael lives on.

As the dedication for the offering was on his behalf and according to his wishes, there will be a harvest of blessings for Michael in his ongoing journey. In Western terms the electric sewing machine is of little economic value. But to this poor family it is the means to having a stable income and regular food on the table.

Review

Most religious and spiritual traditions have the idea of Judgement and the necessity to appraise ones life before and after death. This is part of the process that determines how one experiences the Afterlife, where one will go and for how long. Personally, I like to feel that Judgment is an internal event and that there is no external judge or executioner except the authority of our own conscience. However, there are many beliefs and paths to home. No one really knows the Truth except God.

In Tibetan Buddhism, it is thought that as well as a seven-day replay of the experience of death, the deceased will weekly review every minute detail of their life. They tell us that this is experienced with a consciousness seven times more intense than in life. (12)

At a critical time for me when life as I knew it was dying, I had a personal life-review experience very much like how they describe.

I came home from work very tired, unable to do anything but lie on the couch. As I rested, a large movie-like screen appeared in space, at eye-level, three feet in front of me. My open gaze was transfixed on the rapidly unfolding events on the screen. It was my life to date.

Here, in a series of evocative scenes were all the memories from my birth including the people I had met and all the events which shaped my personality, my nature, even my destiny. The images passed very quickly, but I recalled everything acutely. In a heightened state, I experienced myself in the present moment of each and every event that was before me, as though for the first time. I felt acutely how I and the others involved felt in the scenes Only, the feelings were greatly magnified. It was an overwhelming experience and I wept with grief and regret.

When I recovered, I realised that these revelations were part of a deep acceptance and integratation of my life up to that moment. I was dying, as I knew myself to be. I needed to do this in order to move on. I imagine that many must go through a similar experience in physical death.

Don't wait until you die or are in a crisis, as I was, to free yourself of the past. As your loved one may be reviewing all that has happened in their life, why don't you? Spend a little time each day, remembering as much detail as possible of your life, feeling as acutely as possible how you felt at the time when important events occurred. Similarly, imagine how others involved with you might have felt. Feel love towards yourself regardless of what you discover. If you have regrets, feel the remorse and make a commitment to change. Then move on. This is a wonderful thing to do - one of the most wonderful ways you can repent, forgive, let go and move on.

As you review your life, particularly recall the times you spent with your loved one - the good and the bad times, the uncomfortable as well as the comfortable times. Embrace, accept and honour the richness, depth, and uniqueness of the memories and precious times you shared together.

Notes

6. **The Bhagavad Gita,** *is referred to as the Divine Song of God and is also known as Gitopanishad. It is the essence of Vedic knowledge and one of the most important pieces of Vedic literature. It is the story of Lord Krishna. Krishna is said to have lived more than 5000 years ago.*

7. *Tibetan Buddhism teaches that the Bardo is an interval of experience between death and rebirth (this may be reincarnation or life in another Realm). It can also be the term used for an intermediate experience between the various phases of life. For example, we can have life Bardo experiences while embodied, when we shed one out-grown state of consciousness for another, or while going through life-changing shifts.*

8. *This visualisation is inspired by meditations in **The Tibetan Book of The Dead**, and in particular those in the translation by Robert A. F. Thurman. It is taken from the visualisation of the Five Buddha Mandala. A Mandala can be thought of as a sacred, protective circle. It has been used extensively as a healing tool in Jungian Psychology. It is recommended that you visualize all the Divine forms that you are comfortable and familiar with.*

9. *Home is referred to here as the place of final resting and of Wholeness. That is, the place of Oneness with all that is, was and will be. Some refer to this state as God-Realisation or Enlightenment.*

10. **In The Tibetan Book of Living and Dying** *by Sogyal Rinpoche, P.290... one reads,*

In the Bardo of Becoming we relive all the experiences of our past life, reviewing minute details long lost to memory, and revisiting places, the masters say, "where we do no more than spit on the ground." Every seven days we are compelled to go through the experience of death once again, with all its suffering. If our death was peaceful, that peaceful state of the mind is repeated; if it was tormented however, that torment is repeated too.

11.   *See 10 above.*

Forgiveness and Acceptance

Chapter 3

Reflections

Days Ten to Twenty-One

'The acceptance of suffering
is a journey into death.
Facing deep pain, allowing it to be,
taking your attention into it,
is to enter death consciously.
When you have died this death,
you realize that there is no death -
and there is nothing to fear.
Only the ego dies.'

Eckhart Tolle

In the in-between world of the Afterlife, the soul experiences a journey. Whether this is a happy or a tumultuous journey, wherever it leads to is dependant on the traveller's spiritual maturity and how they react to the impressions and conditions that arise. Just as in bodily life, our reactions depend on the health of our ego and how we have matured spiritually. If we do not limit or lose our ego before or at the time of our death, then it, and not Peace, will be our companion in the Afterlife, just as it was the moment before we took our last breath.

* * *

The ego holds the key to our suffering. It is the ego that feels dread and fear. Where there is fear there can be no Love. It is the ego that likes and dislikes, loves or hates, feels peace or anger. It is the ego which is born and which is affected by death. It is the ego, which obscures our Divinity. It is the ego, which veils our Reality. Remove the ego and you are left with nothing but God. With Love.

Sathya Sai Baba teaches us that the ego is like the tadpole's tail. It will fall away when one grows in wisdom. It has to. If it is cut, the poor tadpole will die. So, He tells us not to worry about the ego. Sai Baba teaches us to cultivate wisdom, discriminate, understand the ephemeral nature of all objective things - and the tail will no longer be evident!

* * *

Which Dream?

There was a farmer who lived in the countryside in rural India. He was a real Jnani (one who has achieved Universal Wisdom). Even though he was an evolved soul he earned his living by farming. He was a living example of the Zen teachings, *Before enlightenment, chopping wood, carrying water. After enlightenment, chopping wood, carrying water.*

He was married and after many years, when he and his wife had given up the idea of ever having a child, a son was born to them, whom they named Haru. The parents loved the boy dearly. They looked on him as the precious jewel of the family. Because of his religious nature all the villagers respected and loved the farmer. Life was good.

One day the farmer was working in the fields when a neighbour came running to him, crying "Come quickly, Haru has cholera... Come... The farmer at once returned home and arranged treatment for the boy. But no medicine could help and the child died. The other members of the family were grief-stricken but the farmer acted as if nothing had happened. He consoled his family but told them that their grieving was futile. Then he went back to his field just like any other day.

On returning home he found his wife weeping even more bitterly. She cried to him,

"How heartless you are. You haven't shed one tear for our child."

The farmer replied quietly, "Shall I tell you why I haven't wept? I had a very vivid dream last night. I dreamt I had become a King. I was the father of eight sons and was very happy with them. Then I woke up. Now I am greatly confused. Should I weep for those eight sons, or for this one Haru?"

The farmer was a Realised soul. Therefore, he completely understood that the waking state is as unreal as the dream state. There is only one eternal substance and that is the Atman. (God)

Adapted from a story told by Sri Ramakrishna

★ ★ ★

Lord, help me to see beyond the illusion of form.
Help me to be unaffected by its play.
Help me to have peace always.

★ ★ ★

When the initial confusion of death subsides and the subtle body becomes stronger in its new energy form, the ongoing soul, which is clothed with a dominant ego will face many ordeals as it journeys through the Afterlife. Strong reactive emotions and feelings will always cause problems. Some Spiritual and religious traditions teach of how the disembodied being may meet with demons and devils. But is it not our own negativity that is the real demons and devils we need to face? Hell and Heaven are not merely something out there. Think about it. Is not what happens in our minds the stuff of Heaven or Hell?

★ ★ ★

Some years before I met Sai Baba, Papaji, (H.W.L. Poonja), the Realised Master from Lucknow, now deceased, took me under his wing for nearly two years. I had been very ill. In his presence and care, I grew well and strong. One day, someone asked him,

"Papaji, what is Hell?

Papaji laughed. "Hell is the mind turned outward and saying I am the body. How can you have peace when the mind decides that everything is only the body. Everybody is going to die!"

Another question, "Papaji. What is Heaven? "

"The mind turned inward is Heaven. As it says in the Bible, the kingdom of Heaven is within."

"How do we win the kingdom of Heaven Papaji?"

"Surrender to awareness. This is Heaven."

* * *

Still on the subject of demons and what they really are, my beloved Guru, Sri Sathya Sai Baba says:

…'One should be grateful all his life to anyone who has helped him in a crisis. Only the man who shows such gratitude can be termed a human being. The ungrateful man is a demon. The human and the demonic are not different in external appearance. It is by his actions that one called human, demonic or divine. All those who indulge in bad thoughts, bad speech, and wicked acts are described as demons. Equally, those who do harm to those who have helped them were regarded as demons.'

* * *

Lord, let me have gratitude, gratitude, gratitude. Let me never forget to be grateful for every moment You have given to me. Let me honour all who have helped me in any small way. Let me Love and appreciate all who have harmed me. What wonderful teachers they have been! Lord, let me see the Divine goodness in all sentient beings. Let me see the beauty in all Creation. Dear God, let me be grateful to You for ever Amen.

* * *

In the Bardo, your loved one's soul may hover around their body and familiar places and people for some days. It is thought by many spiritual traditions that after this time, the soul journeys to a place of Judgement where a decision is made as to whether they will be punished or rewarded. (12) They also teach that the soul-body will meet with experiences and challenges according to how it has lived its life, even before Judgement decides where it will next reside. There are alarming texts in some of these treatises. One such passage in the **The Garuda Purana** reads:

'Those who are well-learned,
who don't incite or cause violence,
who usurp nobody's share,
who remain contented with their spouse,
who are averse to worldly allurements,
who feelingly perform all the post-mortem duties
towards their deceased ancestors,
who duly discharge their familial duties
and repay their dues
and avoid the company of the wicked

are also allowed access to the city (heavenly)
through the West gate.
They reach the gate and imbibe nectar
before proceeding to the Yama's assembly.
(the place of Judgement).'

The Garuda Purana goes on to say,

…'As I have already told, those men with no faith
and weak convictions go to Hell. They are fools who even
after getting this very rare human form
fail to take advantage of it to improve their status
in the Divine Realm.
On the contrary, they further degrade themselves
by getting drawn to worldly allurements.
A man who follows the righteous and honest path
not only improves his present life
but his status in the next as well.'

* * *

Do you believe the notions of Judgment, punishment and
reward to be an external or an internal authority? It is certain
that we have within us deep concepts of guilt, conscience and
Judgement. Many people fear death for these reasons alone.

But we also know that what we believe in determines our
reality. If we believe that we will be judged, we will expect
to be judged. If we believe in punishment, we will expect to
be punished. If we believe that we will be rewarded, we will
expect reward. If we believe that there is no such thing…

* * *

'Even the most heinous sinner,
can quickly cleanse his heart
and become pure,
by surrendering to the Lord
in anguished repentance.'

Sri Sathya Sai Baba

★ ★ ★

Discuss with your beloved the idea of Judgement and how it may be a mere concept in their own mind. The Creator, God, is All Loving. Punishment and reward is something that the mind has chosen to invent and use. But, you and your beloved are more than the mind. You are more than anything the mind can conjure. Tell them that they are indeed the Master of their mind and not its slave - that if the idea of Judgement comes into their mind, to not follow it. When you find yourself judging yourself or others, stop it! It is a pattern that you can let go of.

★ ★ ★

With awareness and remorse, you can squash the fated negative concept of judgment and importantly that of punishment too. Remorse is a greater force than punishment - and more compassionate. If you recognize that you have done something you are aware was wrong, feel as much regret as you can and pray for the guidance and strength to never repeat it. Let the regret go. Don't hang onto it for too long. Remaining in the Purgatory of regret and remorse, is another Hell that is unnecessary. Forgiving yourself and others annihilates the need to suffer in any kind of Hell. Use humour if you can. Humour makes demons run away. Laughter breaks through negative thought patterns quickly no matter how solid or old they are.

* * *

'I am ready to meet my Maker.
Whether my Maker is ready
for the ordeal of meeting me is another matter!'

Winston Churchill on his 75th birthday

* * *

I Forgive You, But...

Here is a well-known parable of a man who lay on his deathbed. He was fortunate that he had a lot of time to think before death came. The dying man had time to make amends. For several years he had stopped all communication with a friend who had treated him unfairly. He had never forgiven him. He realised that he should not die holding such a grudge.

The dying man decided to make peace with his estranged friend and to tell him that all was forgiven and forgotten. He called for him and when the estranged friend arrived, the dying man joyfully embraced him.

He told him, "Soon I will die. But, I wish to tell you that I completely absolve you of all the wrongs you did to me and I bear no grudge against you. I forgive you for everything that has happened."

The friend was very moved. A terrible weight was lifted from his heart. His eyes flowed with tears of gratitude. How good it was, he felt, to be so forgiven and for this peace now between he and his dying friend.

But, as he happily left, the dying man shouted to him, "I forgive you only if I die. If I recover, I never want to see you again and I take back every word!"

Adapted from a story told by J. P. Vaswani

★ ★ ★

The Realms in the Afterlife are as dualistic (split and relative) as the Earth Realm. In duality we experience opposites, a separation from Wholeness and Oneness. This split creates tension and the qualities of desire and repulsion. This split makes us choose something or some people, rather than others. There is no end to these experiences in the world of duality. We can be trapped forever in this *play* of atraction and repulsion.

The play of duality means separation from Wholeness! In order to find the true kingdom of Heaven, the state where there is no birth or death, disease or suffering, we need to separate from duality and experience the balance that lies between the split of the two - a state where we neither seek nor repel. When we achieve this we are One with God. That is, we become One with all that is. We are no longer split. We are Whole. There ceases to be, a you and I, a we and me and a here and there. All becomes One. This is not something we can force to happen. It happens spontaneously when we let go of every desire and repulsion we identify with. When we are empty, we receive everything.

★ ★ ★

Thoughts and imaginations that arise from the ego-mind are not solid experiences. They only appear to be. Tell your loved one, tell yourself, that whatever you see or think, is a construct of your mind, which you can choose to follow or not.

★ ★ ★

'The mind can make a Heaven out of Hell
or a Hell out of Heaven.'

John Milton

★ ★ ★

Jesus taught us about Heaven within us. He did not speak of Judgement or of the need to suffer punishment or an eternal Hell. Jesus told the dying thief on the cross that he would be with Him in Paradise today. It would appear that, like the dying thief, one does not even have to wait... Your loved one can be in Heaven right now. Tell them again and again that

Paradise is within, here and now. Peace, contentment and happiness are within their grasp. Tell them too, that there is a Love even beyond Heaven… There is no limit. Only the mind limits.

★ ★ ★

'Jesus replied,
"There is no sin in reality!
It is you who create sin,
when you do deeds, such as adultery,
that are called sinful.

That is why Good enters your heart
to return you back to your source

This is why you get ill
and eventually die;
he who understands,
let him understand.'

Mary Magdalene

★ ★ ★

Now, we may not be able to sustain a belief that punishment is an illusion in the face of anguish or terror. It is easy to believe that we are being punished when we feel pain or when something bad happens to us.

In death, as the subtle body becomes stronger it is endowed with psychic abilities and with the facility to manifest and to move as instantly as a thought. The soul takes its ego-body of repulsions and desires with it when it leaves the body. Although it can create objects of its enjoyment by merely thinking about them it also takes its anxieties and fears.

Think deeply about the following... Whatever the soul-body can imagine can unconsciously and consciously manifest as quickly as a thought. Negative habitual thought patterns as well as pleasant ones. Whatever, whoever the soul-body is attached to, is the means to suffering.

★ ★ ★

'He who binds to himself a joy
doth the winged life destroy.
But he who kisses the joy as it flies
lives in eternity's sunrise.'

William Blake

★ ★ ★

We, all of us, you and your beloved have to make a determined effort to remember that not all is as it seems. In Truth, nothing and no one can harm us. Tell yourself that in Truth, your Self is perfect and akin to God. That, in Truth, your fears are nothing but fantasies and they can fall away just as quickly as your mind conjured them up. Get into the habit of believing this instead!

★ ★ ★

'Hey noble one! Listen without wavering! …
The white light of the Mirror wisdom,
purity of the form aggregate, white and piercing,
bright and clear shines from the heart
of the Vajrasattva couple (13) before you,
penetrating, unbearable to your eyes.
At the same time the soft smoky light of the Hells shines
before you in parallel with the wisdom light.
At that time, under the influence of hate you panic,
terrified by that brilliant white light and you flee from it.
But now you must fearlessly recognise that brilliant,
piercing dazzling, clear light as wisdom.
Be gladdened by it with faith and reverence!
Pray, and increase your Love for it, thinking,
"It is the light of the compassion of Lord Vajrasattva!
I take refuge in it!" It is the Lord Vajrassattva's shining
upon you to escort you through the terrors
of the in-between.'

The Tibetan Book of the Dead

★ ★ ★

Look to The Light always. Read aloud the above text, this
book, again and again. Read it out to your beloved, using
appropriate words and names of forms relating to their
beliefs. A Christian can substitute Vajrasattava for Jesus,
a Muslim for Allah, a Hindu can visualise Shiva. Instruct
them to connect with their idea of God, no matter what other
images arise in their minds. Ask them to let go of the idea
of their separate-self and completely dissolve into God's light
and Love.

★ ★ ★

'To fear death is nothing
other than to think oneself wise when one is not.
For it is to think one knows what one does not know.
No one knows whether death may not
even turn out to be the greatest blessing of human beings.
And yet people fear it
as if they knew for certain it is the greatest evil.'

Socrates

* * *

People around you may get edgy or frustrated. In emotionally heightened times, a lot of hyper negativity can be flying around. Remember that when someone hurts you, it is really not personal... In fact, it is not really anything much to do with you at all. It does however say a great deal about them.

* * *

Similarly, your reactions are your own. Your thoughts, words, actions and reactions say a lot about you. Be a witness. Do not judge what you find in the mirror. Try not to judge what you see in others too. Use your insights as constructive tools to become more detached and freer from emotional reactions and mental harassments.

* * *

'Father forgive them, for they know not what they do.'

Jesus

★ ★ ★

In this heightened and intense time, when your emotions are more accessible, surrender what remains in the grip of jealousy, resentment, anger and fear. Be wise. Why be jealous in the face of Death? Why be angry when everyone and everything will come to dust? Why hold resentment when all who are born will suffer like you, and experience pain, loss and death? You have been born into the mouth of death. Why feel fear when the worst has already happened?

★ ★ ★

If you are experiencing a lot of pain, try, as suggested by Tolle at the beginning of the section to turn your attention towards your grief. There is psychic pain as well as physical. It is likely you are experiencing both. Your pain is very personal. Others may be able to empathise, sympathise with you. But no one can really feel what you are feeling. Consciously experience all that there is to do with this pain and enter the very nucleus of it. Relax into it. Do not fight it. Be aware if you can, of the space within the centre of the pain. Unbelievably, there is peace there. Share this experience with your loved one. Write them letters telling them what you are discovering.

★ ★ ★

Take the responsibility to create space for yourself. Choose space. When we grieve we sometimes fill every piece of space so that we don't have the room in which to feel what is going on. But you need to feel what is going on. Feel yourself hurt. Face the worst. In facing the reality of this death, you can come to terms with it. You will come to a point where it will change. This will not happen unless you stay with it and you feel every little bit of the pain. When you do this, your soul will ripen into grace. You will become gentle, humble, sensitive, and compassionate for you and others. You will become peaceful. You will surrender. You will accept and you will continue to Love.

* * *

If your pain persists and feels unbearable, use it as a tool of compassion. A great Tibetan Master, Lama Zopa Rinpoche, taught this method to me. It is a way to relax and allow pain to be present without resistance. Here we welcome the pain rather than push it away. When we push away we make things worse. When we relax, miracles can happen. Pray, "I accept my suffering. As I embrace my pain and my discomfort, at least let me take the suffering of other beings as my own and free them of their pain. Let me suffer for them instead."

When I have done this practice with full integrity, I have found that in spite of my desire to take on more suffering, my pain is alleviated almost immediately. It disappears. In its place I find peace. When this happens I pray that the pain of others is at once released also.

* * *

'The body is said to be the tabernacle of God.
The world is the body of God.
A pinprick on the two is immediately recognized
as an injury to the self
because the toe is part of the self-same body.
So too, suffering in one corner of the world
is as much the concern of the Lord as suffering in any other.'

Sri Sathya Sai Baba

* * *

Animals grieve just like you do when their kin dies or when a human caretaker leaves them. But they cannot understand or express what is happening to them as you can. It is only a human being that can enter pain and go beyond it into Divinity.

As a precious human being you can ritualise your grief. You can pray. You can forgive. You can regret. You can accept. You can consciously surrender your suffering to a Higher Authority. You can deeply change. This is indeed something to be truly grateful for.

* * *

The Ivory Bangles

Do what feels right for you as long as no one is hurt. There is no norm. Love has nothing to do with societal expectations. Sri Ramakrishna Paramahansa (A renouned Indian Saint) passed away in 1883, leaving his wife, Sharada Devi, who was known as the Holy Mother, a widow.

According to the customs of that time, widows could not wear bangles on their arms or any other jewellery. Sharada Devi immediately decided to remove the ivory bangles she had worn since she married Sri Ramakrishna as a child-bride. Now she found that they would not come off, no matter how hard she tried.

Finally, she decided to break them. She took a heavy hammer and was about to strike them when she heard a voice calling to her, "Sharada... Sharada... What are you doing?"

It was the voice of her husband, Sri Ramakrishna. "I have not died, Sharada," he continued. "I have but moved from one room to the another."

The Mother let her bangles remain where they were as well as some other jewellery.

* * *

Interestingly, when Sri Ramakrishna was alive, he already set the stage by telling his disciples the following story.

The Gold Bangles

A certain devout lady, who was also a devoted wife, lived in the household serving her husband and children with a loving heart and at the same time keeping her mind fixed on the Lord. On the death of her husband, as soon as the cremation was over, she broke her glass bangles and replaced them with a pair of gold bracelets.

People wondered at her unnatural and disrespectful conduct, but she explained to them, "Hitherto, my husband's body had been fragile like the glass bangles. That ephemeral body is gone. He is now like one unchangeable and full in every respect. His body is no longer fragile. So I have discarded the fragile glass bangles and worn ornaments of a permanent nature."

★ ★ ★

Continue communicating with your beloved as much as you can but at the same time try not to hold onto them. As you communicate, remember that your duty is to help set you both free. Souls can remain earth-bound for a long time because they cannot leave their dear ones behind. They may also remain because their loved ones cannot bear to let them go. It is imperative that you do not pine for them to stay with you. They cannot. They should not. It is crucial that you happily allow them to move on and be free. Cultivate non-attachment as much as you can by concentrating on the happiness of your dear one rather than your own.

Visualise saying goodbye, as you wave happily to your

dear one. Imagine a stunning ship waiting for them. See your beloved walk on board. You both feel excitement and joy. Look far into the horizon. It is dawn and the ocean is incredibly beautiful. Your beloved is embarking on the most wonderful adventure... Use this scene, or something similar as a meditation - a practice to help you let go.

* * *

'Now you feel how nothing clings to you;
your vast shell reaches into endless space,
and there the rich, thick fluids rise and flow.
Illuminated in your infinite peace,
a billion stars go spinning through the night,
blazing high above your head.
But in you is the presence that will be,
when all the stars are dead.'

Rainer Maria Rilke

* * *

Dear One,
hear me!
Try not to get involved in comforting yourself
in this in-between world
which is as temporary
as the one you left behind.

Remember that we create our destiny
through our thoughts and deeds.

Let us commit to the highest Truth
and seek the highest Light.
I am with you all the way
in contemplating God and the Divine.

Let us leave the illusion
of the temporary nature
of worlds and things
and wish for the perfection of
everlasting peace -
our birthright.

* * *

'Various Saints had endless troubles in their lives
with family, harsh treatment from others and so on.
But their faith in God remain untouched...
They themselves did not suffer.
Jesus did not suffer.
But it was necessary that they go through
what is generally regarded as suffering so that
the world could have noble examples of worldly detachment
and unshakeable faith in God.'

Sri Sathya Sai Baba

* * *

Dinah gives a moving account of the experience of her mother's death and of the healing and forgiveness that encompasses generations.

Ruth's Liberation

My mother held on to life for three and a half years in the Nazi death camps. Throughout her remaining fifty years she often expressed her wish to die, even attempting suicide several times, yet a part of her clung on to life tenaciously. In the camps she had learnt to survive no matter how bad things became.

My relationship with her was very difficult. I was diagnosed with clinical depression during my teenage years. The awareness I reached through decades of psychological training, therapy, and a spiritual quest, led me to a point where I was able to love my mother wholeheartedly. However I needed to set strong boundaries to protect myself from the abusive Love which arose from her pain. Sometimes this meant long periods of physical separation.

In 1995 she was diagnosed with diminishing renal function. At first she strongly resisted dialysis. She told me that she finally succumbed to the treatment as a result of pressure from her specialist and my brother. I suspect however that once she realized that she was, in fact dying, she automatically resorted to her need to defy death no matter what.

She summoned me to her home in August 1997. That day she apologized to me for her inability to be a 'good' mother. This was the first time she had ever acknowledged that she had in any way contributed to the difficulties we had experienced during our forty-seven year relationship. That afternoon we came together in love, a wounded mother and her wounded daughter. The pain of our turbulent relationship simply dissolved with our tears as we embraced with open hearts. I knew she was ready to die.

Two months later she was not coping with her dialysis treatment. I sat with her and explained that she actually had a choice – to continue suffering whilst struggling to hold on to a life that failed to give her joy, or to terminate treatment and face death.

After some days she rang me to tell me she had terminated treatment. She was hospitalized two days later. When I found her in the hospital I asked her if she was afraid. She shrugged her withered shoulders. I stroked her hand and assured her I would be with her during her transition. This seemed to offer some comfort.

I was with her for much of the time during her remaining five days. I was able to assist in bathing her just as she entered the comatose state. Whilst holding her shrunken body, I mentally thanked her for having cared for me when I was as helpless as she was now. Three hours later her breathing entered the last stage.

"I Love you mum. It's time to go now. Just let go" And she did. She went without a struggle. At last she had found the peace that had eluded her throughout her troubled life.

She visits me sometimes in my dreams. I see before me a radiant woman. She says to me. "I am so very, very happy. I love you very much."

And at last I know that she does.

★ ★ ★

'As we live through thousands of dreams
in our present life,
so is our present life only one
of many thousands of such lives
which we enter from the other more real life
and then return to after death.
Our life is but one of the dreams
of that more real life, and so it is endlessly,
until the very last one,
the very real, the life of God.'

Count Leo Tolstoy

★ ★ ★

What You Can Do

Happy Stories and Poems.

Read aloud, or silently, keeping the thought of your loved one in your heart. Read joyful, spiritually positive words, stories and uplifting poems. Connect heart-to-heart.

If you feel frustration or sadness in your beloved, ask them to listen to the positive words you are reading. Remind them of the need to stay hopeful, positive and happy and with Divine thoughts of God and compassion, Love and goodness.

If you are depressed, it is difficult to be open to The Light. You are more likely to run away from it. Can you remember a time when you felt low, depressed or angry and you wanted to push someone very loving away, someone who met you as bright or happy? In the same way, if your loved one is unhappy, they may try to recoil from intense loving and light energies.

In the Afterlife, if one is angry or hurt, one may veer towards dark and unhappy experiences. If you feel that there is discord within your loved one, pray earnestly to God and all the Guardians and Angels of Light, to help them be free of emotional shadows imprisoning them.

Express Your Grief

Some people get caught in their grief for a lifetime or even lifetimes because they cannot move on to a place of resolution within them. When grief is repressed, the symptoms can be extremely destructive. Depression, anger, bitterness, chronic illness, even death can be the result of withholding or denying our grief.

Express, paint, sing, cry, write… Do anything that helps you to release the immense pain that is within you at this time. Find what helps you to release your feelings, whilst at the same time allows you to feel held. Talk to an objective sympathetic friend or counsellor. If you want to express your feelings in say, an unsent letter parent yourself by giving yourself boundaries of time in which to do this. Contain times of release within boundaries of time and you will feel safe and held.

Let go of Anger, Resentment and Jealousy

Grief may also be coloured by other destructive emotions and feelings. Do you hold animosity, anger, jealousy or resentment towards anyone or yourself? Do you hold any of these feelings towards the deceased? Negative qualities distance us from others and block the flow of life force and Divine connection. You may feel very tired. Your body may ache. If so, these may be filled with the pains of your unexpressed grief.

If your beloved had no time to prepare for death and to consider forgiveness towards themself or others, urge them to consciously let go of any negative feelings they may hold. Remind them to feel compassion for themselves and others, no matter what has gone before. Ask them to forgive.

Forgiveness

Everyone, good and bad, holy and depraved, rich and poor, celebrated and unknown, suffers and will suffer the wheel of existence of birth, sickness, loss, old age and death. All will continue to do so until they are freed from this cycle. When one realises that this is the fate of all, there is no need to feel resentment, jealousy or anger.

Being aware of this Truth makes it very much easier to cultivate compassion for others and oneself. Let us cultivate compassion and mercy for all sentient beings including ourselves. This is our true nature. The nature of The Divine.

The Divine Image

To Mercy, Pity, Peace and Love
all pray in their distress;
And to these virtues of delight
return their thankfulness.

For Mercy, Pity, Peace and Love
is God, our Father dear,
and Mercy, Pity, Peace and Love
is Man, his child and care.

For Mercy has a human heart,
Pity a human face,
and Love, the human form divine,
and Peace, the human dress.

Then every man, of every clime,
that prays in his distress,
prays to the human form divine,
Love, Mercy, Pity, Peace.

And all must love the human form,
in heathen, Turk or Jew;
Where Mercy, Love and Pity dwell
There God is dwelling too.

William Blake

Sharing and Dedication

Share your deepest loving thoughts with your loved one. Write a letter to them and place it on your sacred table/ altar. If you wish, offer a beautiful drawing or a painting symbolising your Love and the Heavenly Realms as you feel them to be.

Pray that all beings in life and in the Afterlife, suffering from the same difficulties and ignorance you face receive the Grace of God and are released from their suffering. Pray that all are blessed with Wisdom and Peace.

Pray for continuing Grace in the conquest of your own inner demons.

The Four Immeasurables

Recite and dedicate the following Tibetan Buddhist prayer for all beings on all levels of existence, including your beloved This is a wonderful prayer to start to the day.

The Four Immeasurables
(repeat three times)

May all sentient beings have happiness
and the causes of happiness.
May all sentients beings be free from suffering
and the causes of suffering.
May all sentient beings never be separated
from the happiness which is without suffering.
May all sentient beings abide in equanimity,
free from the attachment and hatred,
that hold some close and others distant.

Write a Letter to Divine Love

Express your most intimate feelings at the feet of Divine Love. Who better to hand over your burden to than to God?

God can take anything you say and write, no matter how painful or grotesque. God's Love is the only Love that can do so without Judgement. Write a letter addressed to your form of God. Be as honest as possible. Do not hold back. If you feel angry, express this anger in your letter. If you feel hurt, express your pain as much as you can.

When you finish the letter, read it again and again until you are able to hand it over. Place it on your personal altar or sacred space. Keep it there until it feels right to remove it. When it is time to let it go, burn the letter ceremoniously, symbolically offering it to God, dust to dust.

One letter may not be enough. Write as many letters as you

need to and for as long as you want. Contain your letter writing time by setting aside a period each day of say thirty minutes. This boundary will help you feel held and safe. When you stop writing, go for a walk in nature or do something uplifting like listening to beautiful music or dancing.

Take Some Time Out

Do something enjoyable, something that makes you happy. If you are lonely, find something to do that cheers you, or make a point of being with people who make you feel good.

Read a good book, paint, colour, de-clutter, and clean your cupboards. Dedicate everything positive that you do, for the good of all, including you, so that all beings find joy and are free of suffering.

Meditate on Impermanence and Oneness

Invite your beloved into your heart. Ask them to join with you in the meditation. Contemplate on how everything is temporary and subject to change. Imagine the apparent solidity of your body becoming more and more translucent and finer. Allow your body and your mind to dissolve into your Image-Form of God.

Repeat this meditation, visualising both you and your dear one dissolving into God.

Finally, visualise the Form of God dissolving into nothing. Here there is nothing but Silence and Love. Do this as often as you wish until you feel familiar and natural with the practice.

Notes

12. *Tibetan Buddhism teaches that the disembodied consciousness hovers around its discarded body for around three days. In the Indian Vedic teachings, it is taught that the soul, which passes out of the body is called Preta - one that is marching to the Beyond. Here, it is thought to hover around its body and familiar places for 10 days. The Astral body re-forms and is fully embodied on the 11th day. If the soul is not free and believes itself to be in duality, it will begin its journey to the Judgement seat of Lord Yama, the Lord of Death.*

13. *Vajrasattva is an archetypal Buddha-deity. He is depicted here with a consort. What this symbolism means is that the Deity is complete and Whole. Esoterically, Vajrasattva is the archetypal male form adopted by the Buddha when symbolising Tantric teachings. The essence of these teachings, are unity and Oneness.*

forty-nine days

Freedom and Vigilance

Chapter 4

Reflections

Days Twenty-Two to Thirty-One

'The deep blue sky, the snow-capped mountains painted against the horizon, and the shining red sun sing with joy. You, Blessed One, are my first Love. The Love that is always present, always pure, and freshly new. And I shall never need a Love that will be called "last." You are the source of well-being flowing through numberless troubled lives, the water from your spiritual stream always pure, as it was in the beginning. You are the source of peace, solidity, and inner freedom. You are the Buddha, the Tathagata. With my one-pointed mind I vow to nourish your solidity and freedom in myself so I can offer solidity and freedom to countless others, now and forever.'

Thich Nhat Hanh

This is a crucial time. Three weeks have passed since your loved one died. Some people around you who are less affected by your dear one's passing, will want you to move on and enter your life as before. They may encourage you to do this as quickly as possible. They have a desire to see you happy again - to see you fully in life once more. But you know you cannot. You, life, can never be the same as before.

Your life is still in the throes of a huge transformation. You don't even know who it is that will emerge and re-enter *normal life*. And now you know a great secret - that there is no such thing as a normal life anyway. You may feel more alone than ever before. Stay with here and now. There is nowhere or nothing else than the present. The grace is that God is always present here and now too. The Truth is, you are never alone.

★ ★ ★

So-called civilised life allows little time for grief. In the West, three days absence of leave, one week at the most is the usual time allowed off from most workplaces on the death of a next of kin. There is even less time allowed for bereavement leave when the loss is a friend or loved one not connected to another in marriage. In these cases, usually the time given is an hour or so to attend the funeral.

Other than in the workplace, normal life is also expected to resume very quickly. Modern day life is like a fast speed train. If one is a little slow in getting off and on, one may miss out. One may even lose their ticket.

You cannot help be affected by how your culture accepts your grief and by how much time is expected of you before you stop thinking deeply of your loved one. But it is unlikely that your grief and it's timing will fit in with what present day society expects of you.

If necessary, go beyond the norm. Remain true to you. Have faith in your own process and timing. If you don't, the result is that your nervous system and health may be at risk because of the strain of suppressed tears and grief and the lack of space in which to release them. Do not rush away from your tears. They are normal and healthy. Let them wash away your heartache. They will soothe your heart.

* * *

There are emotional stages that we go through in grief. These stages are usually denial, confusion, depression, anger and acceptance. They are not necessarily experienced in a particular order and people can move in and out of them over a period of time. Severe reactions can come unexpectedly - anger, grief, sadness, frustration, sickness and depression... They may even appear after a period of calm, when you thought you had moved on.

* * *

When I was in my early thirties, I experienced extensive deep losses over a period of months. At the time I was working in a very responsible position for a Government office in Scotland. Each day, I had to put on a face that was acceptable.

I thought I was managing to keep control. One day, when I was standing beside a colleague looking through some legal documents, my body began to tremble and shake. I could not stop it. The shaking went on for some days until I decided I had to address my pain. The body and the emotions cannot be denied. Give space to your grief and then it will not creep up on you and overwhelm you when it is not appropriate.

This was my trigger to enter an intense time of self-reflection, counselling and healing. During the three years that followed, I cried every day. The tears would sometimes come when I least wanted them, like when I was driving on a long distance journey to the north of Scotland to conduct a business meeting. I would park the car on the verge and cry until there were no tears left for that day. After some time, I would resume driving and the work expected of me.

At the onset of this period of years of crying, I would cry for my own grief. Memories would arise also that I had long forgotten and I would cry about these too. As time went on my tears included the suffering of others. Eventually, I found myself crying for the entire world.

I feel immense gratitude for this experience of my tears moving through the small self to the Universal. Even if you do not do anything else that is therapeutic I wholeheartedly recommend that you cry.

* * *

In the Bardo Realm, your loved one will experience and encounter feelings like you, although it is likely that theirs will be more intense. One moment, you will feel that you are in control and in the next that you are floundering. Memories will arise. Unexpressed thoughts and feelings will arise as though from nowhere. These are very early days. It takes time to fully absorb the impact of a major loss. Be kind to yourself. Ensure that you give yourself enough time and space to be with yourself and your innermost feelings. Are you giving yourself the necessary time to just be?

* * *

'When unfortunate things happen in our lives
there are two possible results.
One possibility is mental unrest, anxiety, fear, doubt,
frustration and eventually depression,
and in the worst case, even suicide.
That's one way.

The other possibility is that
because of that tragic experience
you become more realistic,
you become closer to reality.
With the power of investigation,
the tragic experience may make you stronger
and increase your self-confidence and self-reliance.
The unfortunate even can be a source of inner strength.'

His Holiness the XIV Dalai Lama

* * *

You may be exhausted and feeling the strain of having to be strong and courageous for both you and your loved one. Be very, very gentle with yourself. Take care of yourself lovingly in the way you would Love a little, vulnerable child. In the face of so many practical things you have had to do during the last weeks, you have been buffeted here and there. There is no doubt that you are bruised. Look after yourself as the very precious human being you are.

Cultivate humility and surrender. When you have humility you surrender to a higher power, knowing that God is taking care, even of the very minute details of your life. Accept that all that happens is for the ultimate good. We can do our best with the greatest will and determination but we alone can do nothing.

It has been my experience and I know it is the experience of many others, that when one is stretched and pulled to the frontiers of oneself, this ultimately makes one a much stronger, wiser and resilient person.

Do not think about the future or the past. Let these burdens fall away. Do not doubt in yourself. Stay with what is manageable - the here and now.

★ ★ ★

God is Here

Once a bird sat on the mast of a ship. When the ship sailed through the mouth of the Ganges into the black waters of the ocean, the bird failed to notice this fact. When it finally became aware of the ocean, it left the mast and flew north in search of land. But it found no limit to the water and so returned. After resting a while it flew south. Here too it found no limit to the water. Panting for breath the bird returned to the mast. Again, after resting a while, it flew east and then west. Finding no limit to the water in any direction, at last it settles down on the mast of the ship.

What a man seeks is very near him. Still he wanders about from place to place. As long as a man feels that God is "there," he is ignorant. But he attains knowledge when he feels that God is "here."

Sri Ramakrishna

* * *

Amidst the pain and confusion, something wonderful is happening to you and your dear one. Your Love is fulfilling itself. Be resolute and break the spell of any depression and hopelessness. Fight for the Light! Know that every moment you spend doing your best for you and all concerned is the stuff of greatness and Divinity. Do not indulge in thoughts of weakness or powerlessness. You need not be a victim. Dedicate every fragment of progress, for the good of all, including yourself.

'And my ending is despair
unless I be relieved by prayer,
which pierceth so that it assault
Heaven itself and frees all fault'

William Shakespeare

* * *

There is no time for vacillation ever! Life is always too short.

* * *

'This existence of ours is as transient as autumn clouds.
To watch the birth and death of beings is like
looking at the movements of a dance.
A lifetime is like a flash of lightening in the sky,
rushing by like a torrent down a steep mountain.'

Guatama Buddha

* * *

Just like the crocodile in Peter Pan's Neverland, (14) time is being eaten away. Do not waste a moment in negativity. Time is very, very precious. Disengage from what is draining you or which is not helpful to you. Do not involve yourself with anyone or anything that harms you. Every moment of your life is an extraordinary gift. Meet this gift of life and time with gratitude every day. Use every moment sacredly.

★ ★ ★

Sai Baba tells a story in relation to time,

'A devotee wanted to know his life-span so that he could set aside enough time for spiritual practices. He pleaded with God to let him know how long he had to live. Amazingly, God replied and told him he had eighty years.

The devotee was really happy to have such a lot of time. But God continued, "Out of the eighty years given to you, twenty to twenty-five years will be spent in learning and playing, twenty-five years will be spent in home and family matters. The remaining thirty years will be spent planning for the future and for the well-being of your children."

"O Lord," the devotee pleaded. Even in eighty years there will be no time for spiritual practices. Please grant me twenty more years, that I may think of You and attain You."

God laughed and said "O mad man! You do not need twenty years to attain me. One moment is enough. How long does it take to put on a light-switch?"

★ ★ ★

Every moment you are preciously aware of is a moment where-in you can become One with God. Becoming One with God is becoming One with Love. Becoming One with Love, is becoming One with all that is...

★ ★ ★

When you feel pain, accept it as a gift. Pain anchors us in our bodies and in Reality. Pain is an expression of your heart. When you have pain you know that you are alive and that your heart is opening. Pain helps you to stay centred long enough for the winds of change to transform you. Pain is a preparation for your soul's great journey across the ocean of Samsara (15) to Liberation.

★ ★ ★

'This moment is God.
There is only God.
Truth is the same in the past,
in the present, and it will remain the same in the future.
Therefore the time sequence of past, present, future,
is just imagination.
But, "I" am timeless, beyond time.'

Sri Sathya Sai Baba

★ ★ ★

When we leave the body we experience timelessness. Time takes a new dimension. Bound in a body, we are subject to the limitations of time and space. A day in the astral world can be a year in Earth-time! Perhaps even 10 or 100 years or more! Time becomes subjective and cannot be measured, just as Love, Truth, Divinity, connection cannot be measured... Stay connected to Love and you will find that you have all the time in the world.

★ ★ ★

'Now the darkness only stays the night-time,
in the morning it will fade away.
Daylight is good at arriving at the right time.
It's not always going to be this grey.

All things must pass
All things must pass away
All things must pass
All things must pass away.'

George Harrison

★ ★ ★

Trauma, loss, grief, raises more deeply rooted, unresolved pain from the past. When we grieve, it is never just about now. One of the purposes of grief is to help reveal painful and turbulent emotions that have remained long hidden. During these sacred and potent moments of heightened awareness, we are given the key to an ancient locked door. We open the door and put on the light. What we see can never be hidden from us again even if we immediately shut the door. Be grateful for what you are blessed to realise. What you are conscious of is always less harmful to you than what is not.

* * *

At every conscious moment, make a determined effort to choose happiness rather than sadness. When you remember your loved one remember happy memories.

* * *

As introduced earlier, the idea of Judgement and punishment need not be taken as an inevitable Reality outside you. Many people fear for their loved ones if they have died with great negativity or through suicide. They fear there will be retribution, punishment or damnation. At the very least their dear one may be lost, or imprisoned somewhere in an in-between world. Mary and her husband Charles tell of what happened shortly after the death of Mary's brother by suicide.

"My bother was thought to be missing, when in fact, he had committed suicide. We were still unaware that he was dead when he appeared to Charles in a vision. He told Charles he was so sorry for what he had done. He had thought there was nothing after death, but now he knew differently. He had wanted to die to achieve oblivion and release from his problems."

Mary's brother appeared to her husband as sane, fully conscious and repentant. He did this very shortly after his death. He was not lost or in anguish - only sorry that he did not know the truth of death and the Afterlife. Although it is sad that he realises his mistake too late for the life he lost, it is comforting that he is so "awake" and aware so quickly after his death.

* * *

'When through fierce confused projections
I wander in Samsara,
on the light-path of abandoning all fear,
may the Blessed Ones,
peaceful and wrathful, go before me,
the host of dakinis, Queens of Space, behind me,
help me to cross the Bardo's dangerous pathway
and bring me to the perfect Buddha state.'

The Tibetan Book of The Dead

* * *

Actually, nothing can harm or destroy you. If you believe that your True Self is permanent and untouchable, you will perceive all that tries to hurt or destroy you in the Bardo Realm, disintegrate before your very eyes.

* * *

'May I know all sounds as my own sound,
may I know all the lights as my own light,
may I know all the rays as my own ray,
may I spontaneously know the Bardo as myself...'

The Tibetan Book of The Dead

* * *

Waking Up

Many people have told me about their fear of becoming lost after death. They fear that they will go round in circles, be confused, or be stuck in limbo. They are anxious in case they become unconscious and are unable to go The Light. This may be a possibility. But I am absolutely certain that with prayer, it cannot happen. I know this through a very strong personal meeting with a sleep-walking disembodied spirit, who was able to wake up and shine on.

This encounter happened in the 1980's. At that time I was very psychic and was frequently asked by people who were bereaved for evidence of their dear one's continuing life after death. During these years, I met with people who had suffered loss of all kinds as well as those who had died who wished to connect with their loved ones.

From the many evidential messages and happenings, I was left in no doubt of how Love, positive thoughts and prayers can influence different Realties, States of Consciousness and linear time, as we know it.

During one weekend, I had a powerful meeting with a deceased man who was completely unaware that he had died. I had been asked to conduct a Sunday Service at a well-known Psychic College in Glasgow. This meant travelling from Edinburgh, conducting private sessions with individuals on the Saturday and staying overnight at the centre for the Sunday morning service.

I was given an attic apartment in the old, Georgian, main house. The housekeeper gave me supper and left me alone for the night. The house was large and rambling but I was unafraid. Tired from the travelling and the day's psychic work, I went to bed before 11pm. While I drifted off to sleep, the door of my room creaked open and I heard loud footsteps of someone entering. A man sighed as my double bed indented next to me as though someone had sat down at the edge. I tried to sit up but felt incredibly drowsy - almost as though I was drugged. The bed indented more as the man lay down beside me and placed an arm around my waist.

The immediate terror from the weight of the man's arm jolted me into action and I started and sat up. The man disappeared. I became sleepy and drifted into a slumber, and the same encounter happened again - the creaking door, the weary sigh, the indentation of the bed and the arm going around my waist. It was like a film being played over and over with the exception that this time I was one of the characters.

As you can imagine, I sat up most of the night. I was aware that the psychic intruder wished me no harm. It was as though he was sleepwalking and had no idea what was happening. But of course, I did not like the experience. Even so, it was difficult to remain alert. Each time I became sleepy, it was as though my energy frequency changed to one that was in line with his. When my senses alerted and my thoughts quickened, I became more conscious. When I moved out of his frequency into my own, he disappeared. This was quite a psychic revelation.

The housekeeper arrived in the morning to give me breakfast asking me how I had slept. She was shocked when I related the events of the night. "What did he look like?" she asked me curiously. I described him as a middle-aged man of medium build with sandy hair. "Oh, that would be Jimmy, my brother-in-law." She cried with satisfaction. "He died a couple of weeks ago but he came here with his wife recently and they spent the night in this very room. Shortly after they returned home he died."

The mystery was solved. The poor soul was in a dream, re-living again and again a happy heightened experience shortly before he died. Jimmy was obviously unaware that he was dead. That morning, in my address at the Sunday service, I told the congregation what had happened during the night. There was a stunned silence. To believe in the spirit world and want communication is one thing, to experience a dead sleepwalker who does not know he has died, coming into your bed is quite another. However, I used the time of sacred service and the slightly fearful congregation to pray for Jimmy to receive the help he needed to "wake up" and be released from his dream.

About a week later I was at home in Edinburgh, sitting quietly in front of the fire after a long day of work. I was resting in the twilight enjoying the semi-darkness and the flickering flames of the log fire in front of me. Suddenly I was aware of the lounge door behind me opening to the hallway. A bright light shone. I was amazed to see a silhouette standing between the two rooms looking directly at me. It was Jimmy! I felt his joy. I experienced warmth in my heart. He had woken up from the dream. He had left the dream and his body forever. He was happy. Wonderfully, he had come to thank me. "Thank you too Jimmy for what you taught me," I said to him as he disappeared into The Light.

★　★　★

Compassion, Compassion, Compassion... God is Love. God is good. We are reflections of God. There is no need to seek. There is no need to hide. There is no need to go anywhere. There is only awareness and Love... Gratitude, gratitude, gratitude.

★　★　★

'God and I in space alone...
And nobody else in view...

"And where are all the people,
Oh Lord," I said,
"the earth below
and the sky overhead
and the dead that I once knew?"

"That was a dream," God smiled
and said: "The dream that seemed to
be true; there were no people

living or dead; there was no earth,
and no sky overhead,
there was only myself in you."

"Why do I feel no fear?" I asked,
"meeting you here in this way?
For I have sinned, I know full well
and is there Heaven and is there Hell,
and is this Judgement Day?"

"Nay, those were but dreams"
the Great God said,
"dreams that have ceased to be.
There are no such things as fear and sin;
there is no you...
you never have been.
There is nothing at all but me."

Ellen Wheeler Wilcox

* * *

Papaji had been a disciple of the great Indian Saint, Sri
Bhagavan Ramana Maharishi. On meeting his Guru he
attained Realisation. Papaji liked to tell many stories in
daily Satsang. They helped us understand what he meant by
Freedom and bondage. This is one he told about the nature
of existence and death.

In the Mouth Of Death

One day I was driving from Bangalore to my mining camp. I stopped to put some water in the radiator of my jeep. I went to a lake and there I saw a snake. It had caught hold of one leg of a frog. Meanwhile, some flies were coming near the frog and the frog was eating the flies.

I was surprised. What do I do? I could get a stick and free the frog. But the snake is living on the frog and the frog is living on flies. So I am seeing the dharma in this situation.

If I remove the frog from the mouth of the snake, the snake will abuse me. The frog is already half dead and will be miserable all this life.

And I can't save the fly, so I thought it better to disappear from here and not interfere with the world order.

Papaji explained that like the frog, from the moment we are born, we are in the mouth of death. Every minute she is sucking. The moment, which was yesterday, is gone. One more day of our life is gone. The snake of destiny has already succeeded.

* * *

For two precious years I lived in close proximity with Papaji before he died. He taught me about the constant need for vigilance and discrimination, so that we can find and permanently remain with Truth.

Papaji's main teachings were based on choosing total death.

This is the death that makes us immortal. He would tell us that in the world everyone dies only to be reborn. So, really nobody is dying. When there is total death, that is, the death of the ego, we become eternal and are never reborn - never born again into the world of ego, suffering and illusion.

One of the greatest gifts he gave me was the desire to recognise the flimsy veil of illusion that we normally take as reality. "The Reality," he would tell us in Satsang, "is that you are already free. You just don't know it. Remove everything," he would say, "that you will eventually lose. It's no use trying to keep it. When we can do this, you will find out just how beautiful and free you really are."

But, how do we remove everything? Papaji believed that we needed the determination of vigilance and discrimination.

One day when I had the opportunity to speak with him, I asked him what was in the way of my total freedom, "All you need is discrimination. Stay with this and you will reach your destination," he firmly told me.

* * *

Ask your loved one to question what freedom means to them. Ask them to try to feel the freedom they imagine can be theirs. Encourage them to imagine the illusory ties that hold them back from their hearts desire. Remind them that nothing is as solid as it appears, not even who or what they think they are. Remind them to exercise their discrimination and to remain vigilant at all times.

* * *

We cannot own anything or anyone. All we have are borrowed possessions and time. Rejoice in this. For it means that we are in Truth already free.

★ ★ ★

'Freedom is man's birthright.
Freedom is Sat-Chit-Ananda. (16)
Freedom is immortality.
Freedom is knowledge, peace and bliss.
Consciously or unconsciously, wittingly or unwittingly,
all are attempting to own this freedom.
Nations are fighting in the battlefield for getting freedom.
A robber robs for getting freedom from want - though his
movement may be crooked and circuitous.
Every movement of your foot is towards freedom
or Sat-Chit-Ananda...

The real cause is that there is in you the immortal, self-effulgent Soul or Atman, which is one without a second, which has no rival, which is the inner ruler, which is the support for the whole universe. In reality, you are this Atman. That is the reason why you have such feeling and desire. In every heart there is this desire for freedom. Freedom is the birthright of man.'

Swami Sivananda

★ ★ ★

Mary and Charles had another experience of communication with a loved one in the Afterworld. Their account reveals Love in freedom as well as the ongoing journey of the soul.

"When Charles' mother died and my grandfather died two weeks later, they appeared together one night to tell Charles that they were looking after each other. Later they appeared with one another again and told Charles that they had to go on a journey and once they crossed the river they would not be back. We were not in contact with them again."

★ ★ ★

Whatever your beliefs remember that your loved one is still with you through the power of Love. Love transcends time and space. Understanding this will ease you. Look for signs of nearness. Perhaps a sudden smell that reminds you of them. Or maybe a small incidence that feels uncanny. Perhaps a moment of peace as you remember a happy time together. Keep your heart open no matter how it hurts. To hurt is to be alive. Be grateful that you live and feel and that you are not one of the many living deaths that walk in our world.

★ ★ ★

A child in the womb develops what is required to function in this world. During it's life the child will grow and develop the attributes needed for their birth in the next world. When we die we cannot take our limbs or our possessions but we do take our minds and our hearts. Compassion, wisdom and truth will help us function in the world to come.

Dear One,
You are free.
As free as any bird can be.
Fly high into Serenity.
Fly high and claim
peace as your prize.

Dear One,
Be, Be, Be,
without having to try.
Be happy and play
in joy and tranquillity.

When you meet God,
please tell of me, dear.
Help me too
to be free
like you.

* * *

The Death of James

When James died, it was the first time I met Death happening to someone close to me. The encounter changed my life irrevocably. Nothing and no one near to me was ever quite the same again.

I was almost six years old. My cousin James was four. We lived on the outskirts of the city of Edinburgh in a quiet, country setting. James lived around the corner from me in a house on a main road. Each morning he would look out of the window to watch the school bus drive past his door. He got excited when he saw the bus because he very much wanted to go to school. But at four years old he was too young

James' birthday was a few days later than the date set for the next school intake and he was not accepted. He was devastated. His parents pleaded with the school to no avail. James could not adjust to the idea of staying at home when all his friends could join school. When the new term began, James longingly watched the school bus drive past his home every morning without him. He would cry. There was no consoling him.

One morning, not long after the beginning of the school intake, James ran outside his house as the school bus was due to pass by. No one will ever know what happened and why he acted as he did. Perhaps his young mind thought he could stop the bus and jump on it. As the bus approached, he ran out onto the road directly in front of it. The bus had no chance of stopping. The impact of the bus hurled James up into the air and into the path of an oncoming lorry. His crushed little body finally landed on the other side of the road. His mother, my aunt Mary, witnessed the horror from her window. She never fully recovered.

The grief around me was tangible although I did not really know what it meant. I was too young to understand. On the morning of the funeral, James was laid in a coffin in his bedroom. When the adults left the room where the coffin lay, James' elder brother and I crept in to have a look at him. To us, James was only sleeping and we wanted to see him.

There was an atmosphere of tragedy, of melancholy. I looked inside the little white coffin holding James' body. I realised that James who had been so naughty, so mischievous and vibrant was not there. There was only this still lifeless body that did not look as though it was sleeping. We knew something had happened that had changed our entire world. Later, we were told that James would not be coming back. That, he had gone to Heaven to play with Jesus and all the other little children who were not here anymore.

My parents were consoled by the dedication of aunt Mary's Priest and within a few months joined in her religious beliefs, by converting to Roman Catholicism. Their grief and shock was intense. They were also terrified a similar fate could befall me, their only child.

Having converted to Catholicism, I was required to change school. In order to get away from the scene of the crime, we moved from the countryside to the city. Life changed irrevocably. My life became a Hell on Earth. I did not adjust to the new school, or to my city surroundings. The freedom of the countryside was gone. I was unable to go out to play. I was an urban prisoner in an old tenement block with my mother and father as my only companions.

Looking back I now see the immense grace of my childhood experience. Through the challenges and suffering brought about by the severe external limitations placed on me, I had nowhere to go but within. My spiritual maturity deepened as I was compelled to seek inner guidance for comfort. My cousin's death was one of the main seeds of my spiritual life. His life and death and my life were inextricably linked and I feel immense gratitude to him. I shall never forget him.

Years later, Aunt Mary told me that she was glad James had died when he was so young. She saw life as cruel and heartless. She said that it comforted her to know that he had not suffered the trials of life. She believed James was in Heaven. This was the most positive approach she could take from the tragedy. Although her belief eased her pain she was unable to integrate positivity into her life. To her, life was not precious or to be celebrated - only endured.

Seven years after the death of James, Aunt Mary gave birth to twins - a boy and a girl. Patsy and Harry grew into two healthy and delightful children but it was obvious that even with the blessing of twins, Mary had lost interest in life. There was an air of fatigue about her, which was always present. When Patsy and Harry were in their late teens, Mary went to bed one night and never woke up. She had physical health problems, but I believe she succumbed to her continuing broken heart. She was only fifty-four years old.

As I write this, I try to imagine how James' mother might have lived her life, had she been able to accept her son's death in a less tortured way. What would this have involved?

I don't know the answer. But, for the sake of all the other grieving mothers in our world, we need to learn something. We need to face death in a different way from the way Mary experienced the death of James.

The depth of a mother's love need not result in endless tragedy at the loss of her child. This very Love can be treasured and honoured as the greatest force of Creation, a power that goes beyond the limitations of both birth and death and which can never die.

To my family, James' death was a terrible tragedy. To us, he was too young to die but how could we know how old his soul was? He left a great inheritance. If James had lived, it is unlikely that his twin brother and sister would have had the opportunity to be born. His death had a profound effect on my life and growth and I know that it affected many others just as strongly. And so, James lives on through the waves of his deep influence on the lives of all who knew him. In turn, this rippling effect carried on through all of us to those who never met him.

All our lives are deeply interdependent. This book would not have been written and you would not be reading this story without James' life and death.

Let is remember that in Truth, James cannot die. His consciousness is eternal. He only died from the life we knew. I cannot understand the mystery of God. But, I have faith in the mercy of God and God's Divine Wisdom and Love.

Aunt Mary I pray that you can now see God's vision of James' life and death and that you are happy and at peace in their Divine loving arms.

★ ★ ★

The Reaper And The Flowers

There is a Reaper whose name is Death,
and, with his sickle keen,
he reaps the bearded grain at a breath,
and the flowers that grow between.

"Shall I have nought that is fair?" saith he;
"Have nought but the bearded grain?
Though the breath of these flowers is sweet to me,
I will give them all back again."

He gazed at the flowers with tearful eyes,
he kissed their drooping leaves;
It was for the Lord of Paradise
he bound them in his sheaves.

"My Lord has need of these flowerets gay,"
The Reaper said, and smiled;
"Dear tokens of the earth are they,
where He was once a child.
They shall all bloom in fields of light,
transplanted by my care,
And saints, upon their garments white,
these sacred blossoms wear."

And the mother gave, in tears and pain,
The flowers she most did love;
She knew she should find them all again
In the fields of light above.
O, not in cruelty, not in wrath,
The Reaper came that day;
Twas an Angel visited the green earth,
And took the flowers away.

Henry Wadsworth Longfellow

* * *

What You Can Do

Look After Your Body

Physical symptoms usually accompany the shock and stress of losing someone dear. During a time of mourning, we need to pay extra attention to our bodies. Sleep disturbances, loss of appetite, digestive disorders etc. take their toll and weaken our immune system and make us prone to viral infections and other conditions. If you have an existing illness or chronic condition it may worsen with the added strain.

As a counsellor it was not uncommon for me to hear someone in mourning say that they wished they could die. Suicidal tendencies are something different from wanting to die. Feeling that you do not want to wake up in the mornings is not the same as contemplating how to kill yourself. Obsessive thoughts about the deceased loved one are also common.

Lovingly befriend yourself. Be conscious of extreme emotional and physical feelings going on within you. You may need to talk to someone professional, someone more objective than a personal friend. If you have continuing depression and wish you were dead, make an appointment with your local doctor and get essential support. Being psychologically held by another in this way is very helpful until the negative feelings pass.

If you have a panic attack and think you may harm yourself, call a helpline like the Samaritans and contact your doctor. You do not have to go through this alone. But you do need to take responsibility and get the right help for yourself. Usually friends and family can help, but there is a limit to what they can cope with, as they may also be grieving.

Share Your Sorrow

Speak with others who are mourning or who have had a similar experience. Share memories of the deceased. You may choose to join a support group in your area. Grief and mourning are universal but some of the problems encountered can differ with the kind of loss experienced. There are support groups for loss of children, loss of spouse, loss by suicide and other kinds of loss as each kind has its own special difficulties in acceptance and adjustment.

Daily Routine

Try to eat nourishing food and have regular meals. A solid routine holds one like a good mother and father. Routine makes you feel safe and secure. Have enough rest. Go to bed at a regular time. Get up in the morning at a regular time.

If it is difficult for you to sleep, take some warm milk or a soothing bedtime drink. Meditate, pray and surrender yourself to your image of God for the night. My favourite thought as I go sleep is to imagine that I am curled up like a child with my head on the feet of God.

If you are prescribed medication to help you relax or sleep, do not see this as a failure but as a help to you in this time of need.

Claim Sacred Space

Create your own temple of sacred space. If you have a busy diary, draw a small temple in a daily or weekly slot. Honour this time as sacrocant. It is your personal Divine time. Your body is the temple of your soul. You're sacred space from which you draw nourishment from the essence of your Divine Self. This sacred space is a balm for your grief.

Notes

14. Peter Pan is the book based on J. M. Barrie's famous play. One of the unforgettable characters is the ticking crocodile, famous for eating one of Captain Hook's hands.

15. Samsara is the Sanskrit term for the cycle of birth and death, which can only be broken through Self-Realization. That is, shedding the ego and realizing one's Wholeness and Unity with all that is.

16. Sat-Chit-Ananda, meaning God who is Truth, Consciousness and Bliss.

God and Attachments

Chapter 5

Reflections

Days Thirty-Two to Forty-One

'You were never born; how can you die?
You have never suffered change;
How can you be changed?
Unborn eternal, immutable, immemorial,
You do not die when the body dies.'

Bhagavad Gita

God is Love and is everywhere and in everything, every little particle of Creation. God is the song of a skylark as well as the bird itself. God is the sound of the river as well as the river. The breath in everything and everyone in Creation is God. God is the Angels that walk with us. And God is more than all these things. More than anything our minds can comprehend. God is The Great Mystery.

Becoming one with God is becoming one with the Loving Light that creates and permeates all and yet is more than anything that can be imagined. Feel immense gratitude for your precious human consciousness. You have been blessed with the potential to look for God, to find God, to Love God and to become with God.

* * *

Lead me from the unreal to the real.
Lead me from darkness to light.
Lead me from death to immortality.

* * *

'Our death is our wedding with Eternity.
What is the secret? 'God is One.'

Rumi

* * *

More than a month has passed for in your transition. Are you ready to move on - to consider changing direction? To begin to swim upstream instead of the way of all the other fishes in the river? God is the greatest fisherman, the best angler. Once you begin to swim upstream, God will notice you very, very quickly and will bait you to see if you bite the hook. When God lines you in there is no going back. Your ego is as good as dead. You are caught, hook, line and sinker.

Can you see this death as a joy, as something your soul has longed for? If so, you as you have known yourself, will be gone forever. Are you ready now to prepare for true death - the final death?

★ ★ ★

'Transformation must begin with the individual.
When the individual changes, the world will change.
This transformation has to take place in the minds of men.
Right thoughts will lead to right actions.
That is why the Scriptures have declared
that the mind is the cause of man's bondage or liberation.'

Sri Sathya Sai Baba

★ ★ ★

Feeling is healing. Feeling fully is letting go. When a thought and feeling is completely experienced and not just partially, there is a complete letting go of the associated pattern or complex belonging to the pain. Feeling something deeply is the true burning on the pyre. It is the real fire of cremation. Let there be no unfinished business between you and your loved one. When you free yourself from unnecessary ties and bonds, you make the sacred space for the Divine, for something miraculous for you and for all concerned.

★ ★ ★

'The Tao that can be told
is not the eternal Tao
The name that can be named
is not the eternal Name.
The unnamable is the eternally real.

Naming is the origin
of all particular things.
Free from desire, you realize the mystery.
Caught in desire, you see only the manifestations.
Yet mystery and manifestations
arise from the same source.
This source is called darkness.
Darkness within darkness.
The gateway to all understanding.'

Lao Tzu

⋆ ⋆ ⋆

Moving on does not mean forgetting. Detachment does not mean loving less. Surrender does not mean having less power or less hope. On the contrary, cultivating surrender and detachment allows the experience of a deeper Love and awareness than ever possible before. Love and ego cannot be companions. Attachment is the shroud of the heart. Love is One. It can never be two. Love is. It is Love and Love alone that conquers death because Love cannot die.

Without attachment life is simple and kind. Without attachment, our world becomes a heavenly garden of Love and peace.

★ ★ ★

'Who can kill you?
You are afraid of your own Self
and you depend on other selves.
You depend on matters, which are not permanent.
I and you will not save your life.
Millions of time you have been born
and millions of times you have been dead.

You know this taste of death very well.
Now at least start to learn how to live.
You can't save your life. Your body is born to die.
You like dying. Millions of times you have experienced
death, so you like death. You don't like to live!

It's so simple to live.
So simple to be happy, so simple to always be in bliss.
And you simply want death, that's all.
You are converting this love garden of grace
and beauty into a butchery.'

H. W. L. Poonja

★ ★ ★

Love is the most powerful force in the world because it is
selfless. Look at what has been achieved in the world through
Love - at how great beings of Love, Jesus, Buddha, Krishna,
Rama, Allah to name a precious Divine handful, made a
difference to the hearts of millions of people. Humanity has
been touched and transformed by their Divine Love.

Through the power of non-violence, Mahatma Gandhi united millions and his message of Love continues to teach that what the world needs is not power but the power of Love. Martin Luther King had a dream of Love that led to the freedom of his people. The Buddha asked us not just to Love one or two people but to Love everyone, with the same intensity. Not just people but all sentient beings. St Francis of Assisi is a name that is never forgotten because it was empowered with Love. Mother Theresa accomplished the impossible with the same loving force.

The list is endless. These great souls show us how the heart is capable of loving, of how vast and immeasurable its Love can be. And yet, it still seems easier for many to choose the sentimental, the exclusive, the petty, the superficially desirous, the romantic…

* * *

Face your desires and attachments and whatever limits your heart. During this emotionally intense time, they gather together and rise to the surface and you can easily catch them as the fisherman catches a shoal of fish with the net. Your work is to want to see them and if so, you will. If you catch them, they will not catch you. Neither can they drag you to death. Rather, in their death you will walk away from them as a free being.

* * *

Find out now what your strongest desire is. Is it something worldly or is it something spiritual or both. If there is more than one desire, do they complement each other or is there a fight going on between them. Attachment and detachment cannot live together. They are enemies. A desire for worldly expansion is not a companion for renunciation. Preparing for death does not go well with the desire to forget death. Do you want to have more time with God or do you want to have a more social life and friends?

J Krishnamurti observed:

"Most people cannot live alone. Therefore they need companions. It requires enormous intelligence to be alone. And you must be alone to find God."

* * *

Is there a way you can make the space for God and at the same time be in the world? What does alone really mean? If someone is sitting at home alone for days on end and their mind is filled with thoughts and desires, can we say that they are alone? If another is fully engaged in helping others, serving night and day, and yet their mind is fully on God, is it not true to say that they are alone with God?

Ask yourself, what is it that you really want now, for you, your eternal life and for your loved one?

* * *

Just as your last thought before going to sleep can be the theme of your night-dreams and your first thought the next morning, so also your last thought as you die can be the one you awaken to in the body-less state and even influence your next birth. (17)

Ajamila

There is a well-known parable from the Bhagavata Purana. Ajamila was trained as a pure Brahman but became degenerate. He stole, lied, cheated and even murdered. He left his wife and went off with a prostitute. As he aged he begot many children, the last being a son whom he called Narayana (meaning the name of God). Narayana was Ajamila's favourite son.

As Ajamila was dying, he constantly thought about his last son whom he loved so much "I wonder what Narayana is doing? I wonder where Narayana is? Is Narayana happy? Did Narayana have his meal? All Ajamila thought of was Narayana, Narayana, Narayana...

When the messengers of death approached Ajamila he cried out in distress, "Narayana, Narayana." At the mere mention of the holy name of God, the attendants of God came speedily to him and as he took his last breath, carried him to the home of God.

The moral of this parable is that if you call out the name of God as you die, God will receive you, no matter how wasted or immoral your life has been. In fact, saying the name of God is so powerful that without even thinking of God, as in the case of Ajamila, you will also be transported to God's abode.

We cannot choose our death but we can choose to prepare for it as much as possible. You may imagine that you can choose to have elevating, Godly thoughts at the moment of your death. But, when the time comes this is not so easy to do. Strong emotions and feelings take over. Fear, pain, panic or shock arise at critical times, especially in the case of an accident or painful passing. If your mind has been wayward and out of control all your life, you cannot suddenly become the Master of it when you wish to.

* * *

'Man should not die like a cat or a dog.
He should leave the world better and happier
than when he came into it.
He must get away, full of gratitude for the chance
given to him to see God in everything
that he saw, heard, touched, smelled, and tasted.
He must remember the Lord with his last breath.
To get that recollection, a lifetime of practice is needed.
When you are at the steering wheel of the car,
you may be hearing the talk going on inside the car and
even join in it; you may be doing many other things
but your attention will always be on the road ahead...
So too, when you are engaged in various obligations of the world,
never allow your attention to stray from God, the Goal...
So, cultivate the habit of remembering the Lord
with every breath; then only can you remember
Him with your last breath.'

Sathya Sai Baba

Many who had near death experiences have realised that the preparation for death is not something that can be achieved in a weekend workshop or in a few weeks. This is why we are asked to meditate, contemplate and prepare for death our entire lives. Learning to control the mind and be its charioteer rather than its slave will help you to concentrate on God in any eventuality. There is no point in thinking about doing this in the future. We have no idea of the next moment, the next hour or day. We have only now.

* * *

The Day That Never Came

This ageless story is how we believe that there will always be time in the future for our spiritual life.

In a small town many centuries ago, a holy man invited a merchant to join him in daily prayers. The man declined apologetically. "I am so sorry Swamiji. I cannot come every evening because I am a humble shopkeeper and I have no one to attend the shop when I am away." The Swami understood the man's predicament, blessed him and left.

The man's business flourished and he soon became quite wealthy. They met again some time later. The holy man again asked the merchant to join him in daily prayers. "You are so prosperous now," he prodded him gently, "that now you must be a much freer man."

Yet again, the merchant declined the generous offer to meet daily with the holy man. "It's true Swamiji that I have become very successful. But I own so much now, I have to take care not to lose it. Certainly, I cannot leave my wealth in the hands of my assistants. But" he smiled rapturously, "in a few years my eldest son will be able to take charge and I shall have all the time in the world to devote to God."

The holy man moved on. What could he say. He had given the merchant the opportunity.

Years passed and the merchant's eldest son took over the running of the father's business. Once more, he met the holy man and as usual, the Swami invited him to attend the daily prayers. But there were still problems. Aren't there always?

"I am so sorry Swamiji," the merchant cried. "The business has become so great, it is now even too much for my eldest son to deal with and I am having to train my youngest son to help him." The merchant looked a little ashamed. "But, I promise you that in another few years time, my responsibilities will end and I shall be free to join you. O Swamiji," he cried. "I cannot tell you how I am looking forward to that blessed day."

But the day never came. Before their next meeting, Death came and the businessman was unable to refuse to attend.

Adapted from a story told by J. P. Vaswani

★ ★ ★

In the same vein, on the importance of what one thinks at the moment of death, Shree Anandamayee Ma, a great Saint, who died in 1982, taught how the soul upon leaving the body, at once goes according to the state of mind a man is in. "At the moment of death," she told, "one is unable to control one's thoughts, therefore the mind will dwell where it is accustomed to going." Once again, she advised to practise while one is well and strong so that the thought of God may come automatically when one is weak and ill.

She told a very apt story to illustrate her point.

Not A Drop, Will I Give!

An old woman who had sold oil all her life was about to die. All her relatives had assembled round her and were urging her to repeat the name of Rama or Krishna. (God) But she was hardly conscious anymore and could not hear what they shouted to her. Being used to beggars coming to beg for oil, she replied every time, "Not a drop will I give, not one drop!" Saying this, she passed away.

At the moment of death, one's thoughts are weighed as it were. One cannot think of anything but that which has been strongest in one's mind throughout one's life.

★ ★ ★

'Now when the Bardo of the moment before death
dawns upon me,
I will abandon all grasping, yearning and attachment,
enter undistracted into the clear awareness of he teaching,
and eject my consciousness into the space of unborn mind
as I leave this compound body of flesh and blood
I will know it to be a transitory illusion.'

The Tibetan Book of The Dead

A near death experience is like a dress rehearsal for death. How you act and feel at this time will show you how much more preparation you need to do for the real thing.

Similarly, how you are in the face of a frightening experience will reveal to you how you may react at the moment of your death. Can you remember such times? Were you been able to immediately think of God, or say a prayer?

Recall how you experienced those first moments on the death of your beloved. What were your thoughts? Were you able to think at all? This will help you to understand how your mind may act in the face of your own death.

Use this new awareness and insight to help you prepare for the eventuality of your own death. If, during times of severe stress, God or Divine thoughts did not come into your mind, get into the habit now of encouraging God to be present always. Try to recall God with every breath you take. Never let God be that far from you that you cannot call God to be near you in an instant.

★ ★ ★

Having a body gives you a false sense of security. Like the merchant in the story, you may live with the illusion that you are invincible and that life will continue for a very long time. But when you come face to face with the death of a loved one, the false sense of security of a never-ending life is blown apart.

In reality, there is no safe hiding place from death. There is nowhere to turn to, except to That, which we call God.

Remember that you have become embodied so that you can end the cycles of birth and death. This is the purpose of your life. Use your body as the freedom-fighter of your soul.

* * *

'The body is only an instrument and not your true self. The body is a gift from God. It does not belong to you but you have to protect it as an instrument given to you. Everything belongs to God. You have to treat it as a trust and not as your private property. It is therefore your duty to make right use of the body and senses given to you.'

Sri Sathya Sai Baba

* * *

Now, as you move into the last stages of your forty-nine days vigil, you are aware that, regardless of whether you have a physical body or not, your state of consciousness is the same, your reactions are the same, your mental and emotional problems are the same and your joys and sorrows are the same.

When you move from one state of being to another, it is the like moving from one room to another. You take yourself with you. There is no avoiding who and what you are whether you are in a body or not… But there is always the possibility of change, of transformation and of freedom in either state.

* * *

Sai Baba frequently tells His students to place a ceiling on their desires. "Desires are a prison," He says. "Man can be freed only by limiting his wants. You should have desire only for life's bare necessities." He tells us many times, that if you have to desire anything, desire only God.

* * *

At some point we need to face our attachments and desires and place a ceiling on them. There is no better time than now! It is considered easier to do this in a physical body than in a subtle one. One important reason for this is that through the solidity of a physical body and world, we experience limitation.

In a solid world there are karmic laws and time constraints. Many desires are naturally limited. This is how we spiritually grow.

In a physical body, you have the time to grasp the implications of your desires and emotions. You can practice how to restrain them. Imagine what it would be like if every thought you had, strong or weak manifested as soon as you had it?

* * *

Instant Wish - Instant Karma

Once upon a time a young traveller who had been walking a great distance, became exhausted in the heat of the sun. He could not go on any longer and fell at the foot of a beautiful large shady tree. He was very weary, hungry and thirsty. His feet and legs ached. He had no idea that he had fallen at the foot of a very special tree - a Kalapataru - a wish-fulfilling tree. Being near such a tree, wishes are realized as quickly as a thought comes to mind.

As he lay down under the umbrella of the strong thick branches, he longingly thought "Oh, how I wish I was lying on a comfortable soft bed." As soon as the thought arose, he found himself lying on a luxurious bed. He could not believe what had happened. He pinched himself. No, he was not dreaming. How could this be? What wondrous grace!

Enjoying the comfort of the soft bed another thought quickly came into his mind. "If only my beautiful wife was here to press and soothe my aching feet..." As soon as the thought arose, his wife appeared at the foot of the bed, smiling at him, pressing his feet in the most soothing manner. The young man wondered if he had gone to Heaven. He pinched himself again to find out if he was still in his body. "Ouch. Yes, it hurt!

He did not understand at all what was happening but he decided to enjoy himself and make full use of his magic wishes. He was on a roll. "Now," he commanded, "I would like the most wonderful banquet to appear before me to satisfy my hunger and thirst." Instantly a table of delicious food appeared before him. With immense joy, the young man tucked in and relished the food and wine and later lay down on his comfortable bed with his wife beside him.

He began to drift off to sleep. A passing thought tiptoed through his mind, as they tend to do when we relax... "Imagine if a tiger appeared and suddenly attacked me?"

The young man had eaten his last meal. A tiger appeared and ate him.

This ancient Indian parable shows us how thoughts come and go in our minds. It is good to be to be mindful of them, whether they are realized or not.

Adapted from a story told by J. P. Vaswani

* * *

'Eating, drinking, sleeping!
A little laughter!
Much weeping!
Is that all?
Do not die here like a worm.
Wake up!
Attain Immortal Bliss'

Bliss Divine - Swami Sivananda

* * *

Imagine

Imagine being in Heaven and having everything the way you want it to be. You receive all that you could possible wish for without having to wait one moment. It's really beautiful in Heaven. No one ages or gets sick. There is no dirt or pollution. Sometimes there is a little jealousy or envy between soul-bodies but it soon disappears because if someone wants something that someone else has, they only need to wish for it and they can have it too.

Everything is going well but one day you are told that all your good grace has dried up and you have to get ready to leave. "Leave to where?" you ask in panic. You have been in Heaven for 3000 earth-time years. You thought that you would be there forever. That you would never suffer again.

The Angel of Departure smiles with empathy at your obvious panic and tells you that you are very lucky because it has been decided that you will not be reborn as an animal or in one of the more difficult Realms, like the Hell Realm or the Warring God's Realm. The Angel tells you that you are to be reborn as a human being. "Of course, we know human beings have many limitations to face," the Angel of Departure says, "and it is true that you will suffer. But where you are going is much better than anywhere else."

"But, what about my home in Paradise?" you ask. "This is better than the Human Realm. Surely this is the best place to be," you plead. "All my friends and loved ones are here and I have been so happy. I have a nice house and a beautiful garden... "

The Angel looks at you with wide surprised eyes. "But, this place is temporary too... Do you not know this?"

The Angel advises you. "Look, it's not so bad. If you do lots of good deeds and give a lot of service to humanity for a few hundred human lifetimes, I am sure we will take you back." The Angel smiles broadly, satisfied that they have given you a very hopeful answer. "But, what then?" you ask. "Will I get to stay permanently?"

The Angel of Departure shakes their head. "No, I'm afraid this is not possible. Not ever. Everyone has to leave Heaven when the grace of their good karma dries up."

"Well then, what's the point of it all, of anything," you ask despairingly. "Is there no end to all this coming and going?"

"Well, of course, my dear friend. There is every point," the Angel replies, "You are so fortunate. How can you not know this? One day, when you get tired of all this coming and going, you will let everything go and be happy to merge with God." The Angel looks a little sad. "We Angels can't do that. Only human beings can!"

* * *

Use your mind to vigilantly discriminate and go beyond the attraction of forms. Use your mind to let go of the desire for never-ending experiences and immerse yourself in what remains - Pure Love. Attaining Oneness with God, becoming one with the Imperishable, is becoming one with Love. This is what is meant by everlasting life, what is meant by going beyond the cycle of birth and death. Perhaps this is what Jesus really meant when he said:

'I am the Resurrection, and the Life: he that believeth in Me, though he were dead, yet shall he live: And whosoever liveth and believeth in Me shall never die.'

* * *

Dear One,
Hear me!
Are you free?

Do you now see the silliness
of all that has
bothered thee and me?
So many things
that seemed to matter
mean so little now.
I wish I were as free
as I feel
you can be...
I promise you,
my dear
one day I will be.

* * *

Mellen-Thomas Benedict is an artist who survived a death experience in 1982. His story is a remarkable and lucid account of his death. It is not a near death experience, because he died for more than one hour. His account is important for it reveals the limitless eternal possibilities we have in life, death and Love. It clearly shows that there is no end.

What I find particularly fascinating is how Mellen's experience is similar to some accounts of those who have had the experience of Enlightenment - the death of the ego, while in the body. (18) Not everyone has a clear enough consciousness to experience and remember details so lucidly, in life or in death. Mellen is a remarkable man. With kind permission, extracts of his story is printed below. I encourage you to read the full version of his experience at www.mellen-thomas.com where you can also reach Mellon.

Mellon tells us,

In 1982 I died from terminal cancer. The condition I had was inoperable, and any kind of chemotherapy they could give me would just have made me more of a vegetable. I was given six to eight months to live. I began to believe that nature had made a mistake, and that we were probably a cancerous organism on the planet. I saw no way that we could get out from all the problems we had created for ourselves and the planet. I perceived all humans as cancer, and that is what I got. That is what killed me.

So I determined that this was really just between me and God. I had never really faced God before, or even dealt with God. I was not into any kind of spirituality at the time, but I began a journey into learning about spirituality and alternative healing. I did not want to be surprised on the other side. So I started reading on various religions and philosophies.

As a self-employed stained-glass artist at the time, I had no medical insurance whatsoever. So my life savings went overnight in testing. I did not want to have my family dragged down financially, so I determined to handle this myself. There was not constant pain, but there were black-outs. I got so that I would not dare to drive, and eventually I ended up in hospice care. I had my own personal hospice caretaker. I was very blessed by this Angel who went through the last part of this with me. I lasted about eighteen months. I did not want to take a lot of drugs, since I wanted to be as conscious as possible. Then I experienced such pain that I had nothing but pain in my consciousness, luckily only for a few days at a time.

* * *

The Light of God

I remember waking up one morning at home about 4:30 am, and I just knew that this was it. This was the day I was going to die. So I called a few friends and said goodbye. I woke up my hospice caretaker and told her. I had a private agreement with her that she would leave my dead body alone for six hours, since I had read that all kinds of interesting things happen when you die. I went back to sleep.

Suddenly I was fully aware and I was standing up, but my body was in the bed. There was this light shining. I turned toward the light. The light was very similar to what many other people have described in their near-death experiences. It was so magnificent. It is tangible; you can feel it. It is alluring; you want to go to it like you would want to go to your ideal mother or father's arms.

As I began to move toward the light, I knew intuitively that if I went to the light, I would be dead. So as I was moving toward the light I said, "Please wait a minute. I want to think about this; I would like to talk to you before I go."

To my surprise, the entire experience halted at that point. You are indeed in control of your near-death experience. My request was honored and I had some conversations with the light. The light kept changing into different figures, like Jesus, Buddha, Krishna, mandalas, archetypal images and signs.

I asked the light, "What is going on here? Please, light, clarify yourself for me. I really want to know the reality of the situation."

I cannot really say the exact words, because it was sort of telepathy. The information transferred to me was that your beliefs shape the kind of feedback you are getting before the light. If you were a Buddhist or Catholic or Fundamentalist, you get a feedback loop of your own stuff. You have a chance to look at it and examine it, but most people do not.

As the light revealed itself to me, I became aware that what I was really seeing was our Higher Self matrix. The only thing I can tell you is that it turned into a matrix, a mandala of human souls, and what I saw was that what we call our Higher Self in each of us is a matrix. It's also a conduit to the Source; each one of us comes directly, as a direct experience from the Source. We all have a Higher Self, or an oversoul part of our being. It revealed itself to me in its truest energy form. The only way I can really describe it is that the being of the Higher Self is more like a conduit. We are directly connected to the Source.

So the light was showing me the Higher Self matrix. And it became very clear to me that all the Higher Selves are connected as one being, all humans are connected as one being, we are actually the same being, different aspects of the same being. It was not committed to one particular religion. And I saw this mandala of human souls. It was the most beautiful thing I have ever seen. I just went into it and, it was just overwhelming. It was like all the Love you've every wanted, and it was the kind of Love that cures, heals, regenerates.

As I asked the light to keep explaining, I understood what the Higher Self matrix is. We have a grid around the planet where all the Higher Selves are connected. This is like a great company, a next subtle level of energy around us, the spirit level, you might say.

Then, after a couple of minutes, I asked for more clarification. I really wanted to know what the universe is about, and I was ready to go at that time.

I said, "I am ready, take me."

Then the light turned into the most beautiful thing that I have ever seen: a mandala of human souls on this planet.

Now I came to this with my negative view of what has happened on the planet. So as I asked the light to keep clarifying for me, I saw in this magnificent mandala how beautiful we all are in our essence, our core. We are the most beautiful creations. The human soul, the human matrix that we all make together is absolutely fantastic, elegant, exotic, everything. I just cannot say enough about how it changed my opinion of human beings in that instant.

I said, "Oh, God, I did not know how beautiful we are."

At any level, high or low, in whatever shape you are in, you are the most beautiful creation, you are.

I was astonished to find that there was no evil in any soul.

I said, "How can this be?"

The answer was that no soul was inherently evil. The terrible things that happened to people might make them do evil things, but their souls were not evil. What all people seek, what sustains them, is Love, the light told me. What distorts people is a lack of Love.

The revelations coming from the light seemed to go on and on and I asked the light, "Does this mean that humankind will be saved?"

Then, like a trumpet blast with a shower of spiraling lights, the Great Light spoke, saying, "Remember this and never forget; you save, redeem and heal yourself. You always have. You always will. You were created with the power to do so from before the beginning of the world."

In that instant I realized even more. I realized that WE HAVE ALREADY BEEN SAVED, and we saved ourselves because we were designed to self-correct like the rest of God's universe. This is what the second coming is about.

I thanked the light of God with all my heart. The best thing I could come up with was these simple words of total appreciation:

"Oh dear God, dear Universe, dear Great Self, I Love my life."

The light seemed to breathe me in even more deeply. It was as if the light was completely absorbing me. The Love light is, to this day, indescribable. I entered into another realm, more profound than the last, and became aware of something more, much more. It was an enormous stream of light, vast and full, deep in the heart of life. I asked what this was.

The light responded, "This is the RIVER OF LIFE. Drink of this manna water to your heart's content."

So I did. I took one big drink and then another. To drink of life Itself! I was in ecstasy.

Then the light said, "You have a desire."

The light knew all about me, everything past, present and future.

"Yes!" I whispered.

I asked to see the rest of the universe, beyond our solar system, beyond all human illusion. The light then told me that I could go with the Stream. I did, and was carried through the light at the end of the tunnel. I felt and heard a series of very soft sonic booms. What a rush!

Suddenly I seemed to be rocketing away from the planet on this stream of life. I saw the earth fly away. The solar system, in all its splendor, whizzed by and disappeared. At faster than light speed, I flew through the center of the galaxy, absorbing more knowledge as I went. I learned that this galaxy and the universe, is bursting with many different varieties of LIFE. I saw many worlds. The good news is that we are not alone in this universe!

As I rode this stream of consciousness through the center of the galaxy, the stream was expanding in awesome fractal waves of energy. The super clusters of galaxies with all their ancient wisdom flew by. At first I thought I was going somewhere, actually traveling. But then I realized that, as the stream was expanding, my own consciousness was also expanding to take in everything in the universe! All creation passed by me. It was an unimaginable wonder! I truly was a wonder child, a babe in Wonderland!

It seemed as if all the creations in the universe soared by me and vanished in a speck of light. Almost immediately, a second light appeared. It came from all sides, and was so different; a light made up of more than every frequency in the universe.

I felt and heard several velvety sonic booms again. My consciousness, or being, was expanding to interface with the entire holographic universe and more.

As I passed into the second light, the awareness came to me that I had just transcended the truth. Those are the best words I have for it, but I will try to explain. As I passed into the second light, I expanded beyond the first light. I found myself in a profound stillness, beyond all silence. I could see or perceive FOREVER, beyond infinity. I was in the void, I was in pre-creation, before the Big Bang. I had crossed over the beginning of time - the first word - the first vibration. I was in the eye of creation. I felt as if I was touching the face of God. It was not a religious feeling. Simply I was at one with absolute life and consciousness.

When I say that I could see or perceive forever, I mean that I could experience all of creation generating itself. It was without beginning and without end. That's a mind-expanding thought, isn't it? Scientists perceive the Big Bang as a single event, which created the universe. I saw that the Big Bang is only one of an infinite number of Big Bangs creating universes endlessly and simultaneously. The only images that even come close in human terms would be those created by supercomputers using fractal geometry equations.

The ancients knew of this. They said Godhead periodically created new universes by breathing out, and de-creating other universes by breathing in. These epochs were called yugas. Modern science called this the Big Bang. I was in absolute, pure consciousness. I could see or perceive all the Big Bangs or yugas creating and de-creating themselves. Instantly I entered into them all simultaneously. I saw that each and every little piece of creation has the power to create. It is very difficult to try to explain this. I am still speechless about this.

It took me years after I returned to assimilate any words at all for the void experience. I can tell you this now; the void is less than nothing, yet more than everything that is! The void is absolute zero; chaos forming all possibilities. It is absolute consciousness; much more than even universal intelligence.

Where is the void? I know. The void is inside and outside everything. You, right now even while you live, are always inside and outside the void simultaneously. You don't have to go anywhere or die to get there. The void is the vacuum or nothingness between all physical manifestations. The SPACE between atoms and their components. Modern science has begun to study this space between everything. They call it zero-point.

What mystics call the void is not a void. It is so full of energy, a different kind of energy that has created everything that we are. Everything since the Big Bang is vibration, from the first word, which is the first vibration.

The Biblical "I am" really has a question mark after it.

"I am? What am I?"

So creation is God exploring God's Self through every way imaginable, in an ongoing, infinite exploration through every one of us. Through every piece of hair on your head, through every leaf on every tree, through every atom, God is exploring God's Self, the great "I am". I began to see that everything that is, is the Self, literally, your Self, my Self. Everything is the great Self. That is why God knows even when a leaf falls. That is possible because wherever you are is the center of the universe. Wherever any atom is, that is the center of the universe. There is God in that, and God in the void.

I was completely out of time and space as we know it. In this expanded state, I discovered that creation is about absolute pure consciousness, or God, coming into the experience of life as we know it. The void itself is devoid of experience. It is pre-life, before the first vibration. Godhead is about more than life and death. Therefore there is even more than life and death to experience in the universe!

I was in the void and I was aware of everything that had ever been created. It was like I was looking out of God's eyes. I had become God. Suddenly I wasn't me anymore. The only thing I can say, I was looking out of God's eyes. And suddenly I knew why every atom was, and I could see everything.

The interesting point was that when I went into the void, I came back with this understanding that God is not there. God is here. That's what it is all about. So this constant search of the human race to go out and find God ... God gave everything to us, everything is here - this is where it's at. And what we are into now is God's exploration of God through us.

I suddenly came back through the second light, or the Big Bang, hearing several more velvet booms. I rode the stream of consciousness back through all of creation, and what a ride it was! The superclusters of galaxies came through me with even more insights. I passed through the center of our galaxy, which is a black hole. Black holes are the great processors or recyclers of the universe. Do you know what is on the other side of a black hole? We are; our galaxy; which has been reprocessed from another universe.

In its total energy configuration, the galaxy looked like a fantastic city of lights. All energy this side of the Big Bang is light. Every sub-atom, atom, star, planet, even consciousness itself is made of light and has a frequency and/or particle.

Light is living stuff. Everything is made of light, even stones. So everything is alive. Everything is made from the light of God; everything is very intelligent.

The Light of Love

As I rode the stream on and on, I could eventually see a huge light coming. I knew it was the first light; the Higher Self light matrix of our solar system. Then the entire solar system appeared in the light, accompanied by one of those velvet booms.

I could see all the energy that this solar system generates, and it is an incredible light show! I could hear the music of the spheres. Our solar system, as do all celestial bodies, generates a unique matrix of light, sound and vibratory energies.

I was in this great light of Love with the stream of life flowing through me. I have to say again, it is the most loving, non-judgmental light. It is the ideal parent for this wonder child.

"What now?" I wondered.

The light explained to me that there is no death; we are immortal beings. We have already been alive forever! I realized that we are part of a natural living system that recycles itself endlessly. I was never told that I had to come back. I just knew that I would. It was only natural, from what I had seen.

I don't know how long I was with the light, in human time. But there came a moment when I realized that all my questions had been answered and my return was near. Every human has a different life and set of questions to explore. Some of our questions are universal, but each of us is exploring this thing we call life in our own unique way

His Return to Earth

As I began my return to the life cycle, it never crossed my mind, nor was I told, that I would return to the same body. It just did not matter. I had complete trust in the light and the life process. As the stream merged with the great light, I asked never to forget the revelations and the feelings of what I had learned on the other side.

There was a "Yes." It felt like a kiss to my soul.

Then I was taken back through the light into the vibratory realm again. The whole process reversed, with even more information being given to me. I came back home, and I was given lessons on the mechanics of reincarnation. I was given answers to all those little questions I had.

I thought of myself as a human for the first time, and I was happy to be that. From what I have seen, I would be happy to be an atom in this universe. An atom. So to be the human part of God... this is the most fantastic blessing. It is a blessing beyond our wildest estimation of what blessing can be. For each and every one of us to be the human part of this experience is awesome, and magnificent. Each and every one of us, no matter where we are, screwed up or not, is a blessing to the planet, right where we are.

So I went through the reincarnation process expecting to be a baby somewhere. But I was given a lesson on how individual identity and consciousness evolve. So I reincarnated back into this body.

I was so surprised when I opened my eyes. I do not know why, because I understood it, but it was still such a surprise to be back in this body, back in my room with someone looking over me crying her eyes out. It was my hospice caretaker. She had given up an hour and a half after finding me dead. She was sure I was dead; all the signs of death were there - I was getting stiff. We do not know how long I was dead, but we do know that it was an hour and a half since I was found. She honored my wish to have my newly dead body left alone for a few hours as much as she could. We had an amplified stethoscope and many ways of checking out the vital functions of the body to see what was happening. She can verify that I really was dead.

It was not a near-death experience. I experienced death itself for at least an hour and a half. She found me dead and checked the stethoscope, blood pressure and heart rate monitor for an hour and a half. Then I awakened and saw the light outside. I tried to get up to go to it, but I fell out of the bed. She heard a loud "clunk", ran in and found me on the floor.

About three months later a friend said I should get tested, so I went and got the scans and so forth. I remember the doctor at the clinic looking at the before and after scans, saying, "Well, there is nothing here now."

I said, "Really, it must be a miracle?"

He said, "No, these things happen, they are called spontaneous remission."

He acted very unimpressed. But here was a miracle, and I was impressed, even if no one else was.

★ ★ ★

There is nothing you need to do in order to Realise God, that is, to become One with God. All you need is the desire to do this above all else. When you have this intense yearning, all that is in your way will naturally fall away. It is that simple.

★ ★ ★

'The Lover finds the Beloved
and in his arms
forgets the long fever of separation.
To this end then let all prayers be turned,
that God may in his mercy
give us the grace to Love him truly.'

Guru Granth Sahib

★ ★ ★

What You Can Do

Cut Ties and Find Detachment

Cutting the ties that bind us does not mean severing Love between people. It is about cutting the feelings and reactions that get in the way of True Love. We can use this method between one person and another, even between one person and family members as a group. And, of course, we can use the method between the bereaved and the one who is deceased.

Time is not important. If you feel that there are painful or difficult ties binding you with anyone who has passed over even after many years, you can still use one of these methods to help free you both. This method can also help both parties if done within the first few weeks or months of death.

The Cutting of The Ties written by Phyllis Krystal is an extensive and thorough psychological, emotional and spiritual technique. I have used the technique and can personally recommend it. It generally involves two people.

I have developed some simpler versions of cutting ties that bind and I have used these when appropriate. They are helpful when there is not the time for the full exercise or when another person is not available to help.

Three Simplified Versions of Cutting Ties

First Version

Sit comfortably in a chair. Do not lie down. Place a chair opposite you. Imagine the person you wish to cut ties with in this chair. Imagine God, either as a form or as formless and ask God to be present, to protect, guide and inspire you both. (You may picture God sitting to the side, adjacent to the chairs or directly above you).

Keep your eyes closed (this is helpful for visualising), and visualise symbolic ties between you and the one you wish to cut ties with. Allow yourself to be creative. You may, for example, see ropes, chains, ribbons, even glue, or a combination of different kinds of symbolic attachments. You might be surprised at what ties you see but try not to judge or change them. Take note of where the ties are connected to you both.

Slowly and carefully, remove the ties in whichever way you feel appropriate until all are gone. You can be as creative as you wish in their destruction.

When you have fully destroyed the ties, thank the other with deep gratitude for sharing this time with you and for all that has gone before, good and bad. Confirm to them that you are now both free and able to be with your True Self. Pray that you both may continue in Peace and Love.

Offer yourself in gratitude to your image of The Divine, for being with you and for the Eternal Love that is with you always.

Second Version

This version is the same as the first with the exception that you can use the symbolic visualization of cords or strings as the means by which you are attached. (This can be helpful for people who are anxious about trying to visualize what the ties are and who generally feel blocked).

Place the chairs opposite each other with a small table between them. Sit on one and light a candle on the table.

With your eyes closed, envisage the other person in the chair opposite, tied to you with the cords or string. (Note where these ties are attached.)

Imagine the candle flame burning through the very centre of the cords until you are both free. Visualize yourself and the other person removing what is left and place these remains in a bundle. Picture both of you handing over the remains to your Divine Image to destroy them.

Third Version

This is an exercise for people who feel more comfortable writing rather than visualising.

Draw matchstick figures of yourself and the person concerned at each end of the base of a triangle. Write your names above the figures. At the apex of the triangle, write the name of The Divine you feel most comfortable with.

Draw the ties between you that bind you. Again, you can be as creative as possible.

Spend some time contemplating your drawing.

Pray to The Divine that the ties be permanently removed.

Using a pair of scissors cut through the centre of the ties.

With a candle-flame, safely burn your drawing as you offer the whole procedure in surrender to God, asking for peace and healing.

Have gratitude to The Divine and to the one you have cut ties with, for the Peace and healing you now have.

Dinah, who gave a personal account earlier about the experience of her mother's death, used the cutting of the ties with her deceased father.

Go To The Light

My father always presented an optimistic outlook. Despite having lost all the members of his family in the death camps. He was a joker and the life of the party. In fact, he was very much in control - in control of my mother, in control of me, in control of his feelings. Well most of the time, anyway. He, like my mother, experienced periods of deep depression, which were treated with medication. He was highly opinionated and a strict disciplinarian.

He was eventually diagnosed with lymphatic leukaemia in 1968. For five years his cancer was treated with steroids. Eventually he succumbed to the side effects of his medication. He died of renal failure on 15th November 1973. By that time I had been 'excommunicated' from the family. Unable to maintain any level of personal integrity within the regime imposed by my father, I had moved into digs in the bohemian inner suburbs of Melbourne, where I supported myself through tertiary studies.

Prior to my Father's death he and I had an ultication regarding my boyfriend. This was when I was ordered from the house and told by my father that he never wished to see me again. Furthermore I was not to attend his funeral.

When the phone rang at five in the morning, I knew it was my brother with the news of our father's passing. That evening I felt a presence hovering at the ceiling of my bed-sit. It was my father. He spoke to me.

"I know you are a good person. I know you will have a good life. Please be at my funeral. Your mother needs your support." I rang my brother and arranged to meet him and my mother at the funeral parlour.

In 1989 I was introduced to "Cutting the Ties that Bind". This is a therapeutic technique, which frees one from unhealthy emotional attachments. It is advised that the first cuts to undertake are those with ones parents. It is through these primary relationships that our core beliefs and basic behavioural patterns are formed.

One cuts the ties through a guided visualization, after which one asks for forgiveness from the other for any thoughts, words, or actions, which have caused pain. Then one offers forgiveness and thanks for the gift of the relationship. When all this is done one respectfully asks the person to leave one's inner space.

When I reached this part of the exercise during the cut with my father, he simply refused to leave. In the visualization I offered him a variety of vehicles to facilitate his journey, but he stayed put. It was at this point that I realized that he had not moved over. I sensed his fear. He was still trapped in his need to take care of my mother and to be in control of the family. He had taken on these roles to fill the emptiness left by the enormous losses he suffered through the Holocaust. He was trapped in his fear of nothingness. I spoke to him gently.

"Dad, we are OK. We are managing. We are all getting on with our lives just as it should be. You've done all you can. Now it's time for you to move on to where you are supposed to be. There is nothing to fear. Only Love awaits you. Please go and be free."

I felt the shift in my heart. I was overcome with an intense experience of Love as he left my inner scene.

Perhaps I had been assigned the role of guiding my father to the light.

* * *

Dinah's story is of how emotional ties can bind, even after many years. It is never too late to free oneself or a loved one, in life or in death.

Continuity of Prayers and Creating A Memorial

Say regular prayers for peace and Love for you and your loved one. These can be daily, weekly, monthly… Whatever feels appropriate for you. Cultivate happiness. Contentment, happiness, bliss. Imagine both of you in radiant sunshine, filled with joy. Pulsating waves of peace-filled vibrations are a balm to the soul no matter in what Realm of existence.

Make offerings, do good deeds, in the name of and on behalf of your loved one. Request prayers for world peace, in your local church, temple or monastery. This is a beautiful way to help the abundance of blessings flow for all concerned.

Celebrate your loved one's life by creating a memorial for them. There are many kinds of memorials you can create, from a gravestone, to a public bench.

Paying tribute to the dead is food for the deceased soul, symbolically, a celebratory garment which the soul can wear and feel good about. It is also consoling for the one making the dedication. Rituals and ceremonies acknowledge the pain of loss, while offering social support and a reaffirmation of life.

Sometimes people give a special party in honour of their dear one, especially one that is traditional and involves dancing and singing. In Ireland, just after the funeral, there is The Wake where everyone gathers together to honour and celebrate the life passed, telling stories, laughing, dancing and singing. This is something you can also arrange if you feel it to be appropriate.

If you want to do something more private, create a sacred circle - a Mandala, with a beautiful surround. Within the circle, paste special images, photographs, words, and draw or paint symbols in honour and celebration of your dear one's life and passing. Include positive words and beautiful images of how you perceive the Afterlife and where you believe your Loved one now resides.

Similarly, create a beautiful garden somewhere, or plant trees in honour of your beloved, or write a poem or a special song.

Notes

17. *Eastern philosophies of Reincarnation, teach us that our last thought is the focus of and fundamental energy of our next life. It is taught in Buddhism and Tibetan Buddhism as well as in Indian philosophy that the last thought bubble of a dying person is the thought bubble of the next life.*

Usually the last thought one has at death is the one that has motivated the life... This is the way the mind works. It may be the Love of someone, or of money or of fear. The last thought of a soldier in battle is of killing his enemy. The last thought of a miser will be the loss of his/her money.

There are six main Realms or states of mind that are identified in relationship to rebirth. They are related to Tibetan Buddhism but other religions refer to these same universal conditions of the mind and how they create our Realms of experience - external or internal.

Anger is related to the Hell Realm. Avarice is related to the Hungry Ghost Realm. Ignorance is related to the Animal Realm. Doubt is related to the Human Realm. Jealousy is related to the Demi-god or Warring God Realm. And finally, pride is related to the God or Heavenly Realm (from where we have to return from one-day to continue our suffering.

18. *To take an example, when Swami Muktananda achieved Realization, he wrote how, "The whole universe is the playground of Chiti (Universal Consciusness), it is the manifestation of God, is is the splendour of the true Self... It is the expansion of your own Self.*

In the Katha Upanishad, Nachiketa is told by Yama, that his real being is found where, "There shines not the sun, neither the moon nor star, nor flash of lightning, nor fire lit on earth. The Self is the light reflected by all, He shining, everything shines after him.

Body and Rebirth

Chapter 6

Reflections

Days Forty-Two to Forty-Nine

'There'll come a time when most of us return here
brought back by our desire to be
a perfect entity.
Living through a million years of crying
until you've realized the Art of Dying.
Do you believe me?'

George Harrison

Your vigil is coming to an end. You have had the opportunity to fully respect, honour and lay to rest the personality and life that was your beloved. In undertaking this vital task you are more free and able to continue with your new lives. And you will go on. Of this there is no doubt. Until, as George Harrison writes, you are a perfect entity.

When you reach perfection it is certain that you will have achieved the art of dying. You will have discovered how to be eternal and there will be no need to die anymore.

★ ★ ★

Taking God's Hand

Some years ago, not long after I had my first personal interviews with Sai Baba, I had a vivid dream. It was dawn and I was walking along a path towards a great tree with immense branches and thick foliage. It looked like the image of the Tree of Life or The Tree of Knowledge that is often depicted in symbolic literature.

Before the tree and to my left was the entrance to a large open stadium where hundreds of thousands of people were waiting. I realized that they had been there for many hours. I knew they were here to see Sai Baba. My heart sank. I had also come to see Him but I was too late. There was no room in the stadium and I feared the immense crowds. I walked towards the tree and stood near its trunk under its vast, comforting shade. "Perhaps if I stand here, I shall at least have a glimpse of Him as He enters the stadium," I thought, deciding to wait there for as long as it took.

Shortly, a radiant Divine Being appeared on the path leading to the stadium. He was surrounded by a handful of people, who were looking at Him with devotion-filled eyes and bliss. I knew that this Being was Sai Baba although He did not look like Sai Baba.

His features and hair resembled ancient iconic paintings of Christ. Unexpectedly He did not turn into the stadium grounds but passed by the entrance and came towards me as I stood under the great tree.

His smile, filled with Love and radiance, enveloped me. "Are you ready," He said, as He held out His hand to me. "Come... "

I looked at His hand but did not take it. Something within me stopped me and I found myself asking Him, like an innocent child, "Will you wait for me while I get my suitcase?"

He smiled at me nodding his beautiful head and I ran. I ran away from Him to get my suitcase. I arrived at a dark, cramped room and began packing my suitcase, throwing in clothes and items that I thought meant something to me. Then there was another suitcase and another. I was intent and in a rush. Someone came to the room and began speaking to me. They wanted my help. I engaged in conversation with them. Another person came to talk with me about something else. Then another. I became immersed. I got lost.

A long time later, a moment of awareness arose and I recollected Sai Baba and our meeting at the tree. I was stunned. I realized that I had been in this dark, dingy room for a long time, lost in my mind and interactions. I had forgotten all about Him and about our wondrous meeting at the tree. How could I have forgotten Him? How could I have asked Him to wait and become lost in packing suitcases and having mindless conversations with people? I despaired that He would be long gone—having given up the idea of waiting for me. Who would want to wait for so long for such a one as me? I started to run back to the tree. I never got there. I awoke with feelings of panic and fear and deep regret.

What a blessing, this dream turned out for me. It showed me how I, we, get lost in the cramped darkness of our lives and attachments and our daily patterns and connections, even in the face of God. I later saw pictures of Prema Sai (19), who Sai Baba has foretold will be His next incarnation and I recognized Him as the Divine Being in my dream. The dream was a sharp reminder of how unconscious I could be. But it also helped to wake me up. It was an abrupt Godly prod of how I, we, need to be ready at all times to take the hand of God. My baggage was in the way of the most precious meeting and journey I could experience. I realised the true art of dying - letting the attachments die that stop us being with God.

One year later, I was aware of dreaming the exact, same dream. Only this time I was conscious of the previous dream and that I was dreaming it again. I had another chance! I was waiting at the heavenly tree. My being lit up as I saw Him once more walk towards me as Prema Sai. He smiled at me as though no time had passed since our last meeting at the tree. No Judgement... No need to forgive... No need to remind me of my earlier foolishness...

He held out His hand to me. 'Are you ready?" He asked, looking into my eyes intently. I felt such Love for Him. Yet, I found myself involuntarily saying, "Yes, but will you allow me to take a shower and wear white for You." He smiled and nodded and remained as I left. I know He is waiting for me. It is my desire to purify myself, not His. He showed me that

He accepts me just as I am. He is always waiting for me, as he is waiting for us all. I know without any doubt that when this dream comes to me the third time, I will take His hand and leave my present body. It will be my time to die and move on.

* * *

The bereaved may ask, "Will my beloved reincarnate or will they remain in a heavenly Realm? Will they come back to me? Will I ever meet them again in another body? Is there really the possibility of rebirth in a different body and time? Will they survive at all? And if so, what will survive - the personality, the identity, or the soul alone? Is Heaven a permanent place or somewhere temporary? And what does it really mean to be One with God? "Will my child really remain in limbo for all eternity?"

For as many questions asked, there are as many different beliefs and religious or spiritual traditions. Ultimately, The Great Mystery remains and I personally, find comfort in this. Usually whatever man has discovered as a Truth has later been found to be untrue. It is not that long ago humanity believed that the earth was flat! We are but small children in the face of Eternity. And, is it not better to be fully aware of the journey than the destination? Perhaps there will never be such an end as a destination. How do we know for sure? Perhaps the God that we are, is eternally growing amd transforming, as Mellen and some Mystics have been inspired to wonder. Consider for a moment that even Peace, Bliss and Love are still expanding and that their expansion is eternal.

The ancient teachings that are still available to us say that everything is up to us and that everything and everyone is One. We are told that beyond the world of matter and living beings, beyond the many Realms that contain Angels, Gods and demi-Gods, Heavens and Hells, there is a supreme existence, which is pure bliss. This is home, where we came from, and to which we will ultimately return. Hinduism and Tibetan Buddhism and Vedanta pertain to these teachings, but the teachings are even older than the religions, which have been influenced and come into being through them. Even these Truths become influenced by the religion that builds around them.

Man, through the mind, is still groping in the dark searching for illumination. And, as we can see through the diversity of Spiritual Traditions and teachings, even great Masters and respected paths do not always agree on fundamental ideas of death and the Afterlife. Where does this leave you?

This leaves you in an amazing place of discovery. It is you alone that can know what is true for you in any given moment of time. The only way you will find the Truth is through exploring the boundlessness of your heart-wisdom and not through the imprisoning mind. If you go beyond the mind, something else happens and you enter the Great Mystery of what we call God.

★ ★ ★

Inter-Connectedness

You and I are the Universe.
We are also our own private worlds -
Yet the world's heart is ours and we walk on a pathless land,
which is the embodiment of Truth.
We have to find that still and silent point within ourselves,
the point, which reflects the many aspects of truth like the
facets of a diamond.

Ancient Wisdom leads us across the farthest reaches of space
to the margins and the frontiers of the Cosmos -
It is the path, which leads inward to the deepest recesses
of being. Ultimately the journey outward and the journey
inward, both arrive at the end of the other. The Microcosm
eventually makes you fathom the Macrocosm.

We now tread the path where silence lives.

Manizeh Sait

★ ★ ★

Some amazing eternal Truths have been touched on in
this book. Let them inspire you. Take from them what you
need in the moment. Their Wisdom tells us that what we
think, we will realize. That what we believe in will manifest.
Where we think we go to after death, we will find ourselves.
Who we think we will see at the time of death, will appear.
Find out what you believe and what you really think. Who do
you think you will see at the time of your death and beyond?
Why you have your precious human life and what you intend
to do with it?

* * *

'There are two ways to live your life -
one is as though nothing is a miracle,
the other is as though everything is a miracle.'

Albert Einstein

* * *

In seeking the Truth, follow your own inner prompting and directions. If you are fortunate, you will receive confirmation that you are on the right track. Be open to Divine messages coming to you like God's calling cards affirming to you that you are heading in the right direction

* * *

We think linearly. But outside the body, there is no linear time, at least not as we know it. Ancient Mystics and modern physics are now agreeing what the great Masters have always known. That we exist on multidimensional levels and there are levels within levels.

On the simplest of levels, this reveals to me that through the power of Love and connection one can be reincarnated in an entirely different life while at the same time remain connected to loved ones in a previous life or lives. If everything is happening in the now, everything is happening in the now... There is no past or future. This idea is difficult for our minds to take on board but not our hearts.

Sai Baba tell us:

'This moment is God. There is only God.
Truth is the same in the past, in the present and it will
remain the same in the future. Therefore the time sequence
of past, present, future is just imagination.'

★ ★ ★

When we identify with being a body, we experience linear
time. We experience birth and death and therefore, most
likely rebirth after death. On a certain level of Consciousness,
time and timelessness coexist together. When we dis-identify
with being a body we go beyond time, birth and death.

★ ★ ★

If you are not yet merged with God, you cannot help being
identified with the body. But your body can help you find
God. Honour and respect your body and all that it contains.
Look after your body as the Divine temple it is. Have you
ever visited a temple or place of worship that is filthy and
uncared for? It feels sacrilegious to see such an event. Who
would wish to stay in such a place? This is how your body
is when you do not Love it, every part of it, internally and
externally, skin, bones, organs, emotions, everything. When
it is uncared for and unloved, the Divine cannot radiate.

All great Masters tell us to care for the body for the body is the temple of the soul. Muktananda told his students,

'If you want to find Love
you must have a true understanding of the body…
The body has been man's companion and friend
through many births…
The body is a fundamental necessity of Sadhana (Spiritual
Practice)… The body is the servant of the Self…
Your body is a marvellous work of art created by God,
a beautiful storehouse full of intelligence,
a mine of secret knowledge.
To enter the court of God
you are going to use your body.'

Papaji told us,

'Take very good care of the body
because this is the rarest gift that nature can give you
- a human birth.
Take good care of it because it is the temple of God.
God is seated in your heart. And this body will be useful
for higher attainment of knowledge.
Don't ignore it. Keep it very well and fit
up to a complete human span of life.'

Sri Sathya Sai Baba tells us,

'The body is the temple of God.
The life of the person is the priest.
The five senses are the vessels used in the religious ceremony.
Atma is God, the idol of God. One cannot say that the
body is the temple of God unless it is. Every act, thought

and word should be worship in the temple. The five senses should constantly be cleansed and polished, so that the worship is reverently offered to God.'

But, Sai Baba also warns us

'Do not become attached to this temporary physical body. Use the body as a tool. Consider yourself as separate from this destructible body, which has been created out of the blending of the five elements. Know yourself as the indestructible Supreme Being!'

★ ★ ★

If you believe that your loved one will be reincarnated, help them to find a good new body. A good body, a good rebirth, a good life will guide a veiled consciousness more quickly to peace and freedom

In the Tibetan Buddhist Tradition it is believed that the deceased normally experience rebirth within 49 days. Other traditions teach different periods of time. But, what is time? Everything has happened, is happening and will happen right now. If you feel, believe or think, that your beloved is reincarnating, help them to have the best possible rebirth. Help them to be born into a good body and family that will lead them to eternal happiness.

Like is attracted to like. Your loved one's incarnation will reflect their thoughts. If they continually visualise their form of God they will be reborn into a luminous and Love-filled form. They will be blessed to receive all that they need to continue to find God. Pray that their thoughts remain elevated and pure. Read these words to them as often as you can. Help them to have the best possible life with all the opportunities for further spiritual progress and the finding of Love.

★ ★ ★

You may find that your heart is more comfortable in believing that your loved one is in a permanent heavenly abode. If so, visualise them as vividly as you can in the most beautiful Paradise, surrounded by heavenly beings. See your dear one very, very happy. If they were old and in pain or had some handicap, visualise them as perfect, vibrant and whole. Imagine God's light shining on them with a host of Angels gathered round them, singing the most divine song. Be happy and grateful that they have found the most perfect place of peace.

★ ★ ★

Your beloved must shed the garment and personality of their previous life to facilitate their new life. Imagine if today you were fixated with the memory of yourself as a child. Could you be the complete adult you are today? It is the same with a past life. You need to shed your previous personalities and memories to be present to who you are now.

Whether you believe in Reincarnation, are an Agnostic, have faith in Heaven as a permanent abode, or some other concept, it makes sense, does it not, to let go of the past?

★ ★ ★

The snake does not try to hold onto the skin it has shed. It leaves the remains to decay and turn to dust as it moves on revealing a new skin. Unlike some creatures, a dead human body is of little use and is quickly buried or cremated. The personality that belongs to the body dies and the soul-body moves on. Personalities are reflections of our karmic patterns. They are related to the ego and are situational. They have little to do with the eternal depths of our hearts.

★ ★ ★

Have faith that the love of your beloved will never leave you regardless of any future body, personality, or life they take. This does not mean that you should long for them to be with you. You must let them go. But you can do so knowing that in the ever present now of timelessness your connection of Eternal Love remains.

My mother who is 85 years old and is very psychic frequently sees my father who died more than 25 years ago. I firmly believe that he has reincarnated at least once since his passing. But I also have no doubt that his soul-body has visited my mother. This usually happens when she ill or needing help in some way. Or when she just needs to know she is not alone. Time and distance do not matter. Love does.

★ ★ ★

'If you've connected with someone in a moment of Love,
the essence of that person is right there with you
even after their death.'

Ram Dass

★ ★ ★

'You are first a child, then grow old and drop the body,
but you never die and never were born.
In the East, Vedantists believe in reincarnation, in
innumerable births and deaths, until one attains Godhood.
The Muslims believe in one birth only and one death only.
The Christians and the Zoroastrians the same. All are right.
But Jesus, Buddha, Muhammad, Zoroaster all meant what I
mean by real birth and real death.
I say you are born once and die once.

All the so-called births and deaths are only sleeps and
wakings. The difference between sleep and death is that
when you sleep you awake and find yourself in the same
body; but after death you awake in a different body.
You never die.
Only the blessed ones die and become one with God.'

Meher Baba

★ ★ ★

Pilgrimage to Kolkata

In 2006, I went on pilgrimage to Kolkata, the city of Joy, (formerly Calcutta). I had the opportunity to visit Mother Theresa's Mission. I deeply respected what Mother Theresa had accomplished in her life and I thought of her as a great soul. Even so, I felt ambivalent about visiting the Mission. I don't know why. Perhaps it was a subconscious resistance to Roman Catholicism itself and not to Mother Theresa. I had undergone a severe and rather unhappy Catholic schooling. Something certainly made me feel less open to visiting the tomb and Mission of a great soul than I would expect.

Mother Theresa's presence throughout the mission was tangible. But, as my travelling friend and I entered the room where her body lay, we both unexpectedly and spontaneously cried. Tears fell down our cheeks in response to the incredible and powerful Love that enveloped us. It was so strong I felt faint. The reaction was completely spontaneous and unlooked for. There was no doubt that although Mother Theresa had left her body, her Love was very, very, present. My ambivalence flew out the window and my heart opened in the awesome Presence of Divine Love.

A short while later after sitting by the Mother's tomb for some time, we looked round the small museum containing Mother Theresa's letters, a few belongings, photographs and profound words. We had an encounter with one of the senior nuns. The light of Love shone through her eyes. We talked for a short while, but before we parted I was compelled by some inexplicable inner prompting to tell the radiant sister that I remembered Mother Theresa's death very well. It was not only the time of Princess Diana's funeral but I myself miscarried that same day, suffering the loss of a four month pregnancy. The tragedy had affected me deeply and had profoundly affected my life. The nun's eyes darkened in compassion as she felt the depth of grief that remained within me.

"Wait," she told my friend and I, returning some time later to give us a selection of pamphlets and photographs of Mother Theresa. She gave us both a small laminated photograph of Mother Theresa. But, mine was of Mother Theresa holding a small Indian baby as she lovingly smiled into the baby's happy face. The baby I lost could have well looked like the one in the photograph. I noticed a round circular hole on the bottom left-hand side of the picture. "This is a piece of Mother's sari for you," she whispered quietly, because you lost your child."

This short and profound interlude contained the deepest healing for me. It was now 2006. Nine years had passed since the miscarriage but it was as though it were yesterday. I held the little photograph of Mother Theresa to my heart and placed my fingers over the tiny piece of her sari. My grief had somehow come full circle and was soothed. A miracle of Divine timing and meeting had occurred. The connection of Love that is everything and everyone had reached out to me and embraced me through this event. Even as I write now, the small picture of the Mother and child is in front of me, on the shelf of my writing desk and I feel so very grateful for her wondrous gift.

I am grateful that I had not followed the ambivalence of my mind. It was another indication to me, one of many, that the mind knows so little. Only the heart has the power to know and understand the Truth.

★ ★ ★

'Death is nothing but going home to God.'

Mother Theresa

★ ★ ★

In a sense we have come full circle. The mystery of life and death remains. But is it not wonderful to not have all the answers? Is it not exciting to be able to trust in the unknown, aware that something wonderful is happening? Life and death is indeed a journey of discovery. The journey of the Self is the discovery of God.

★ ★ ★

'Our birth is but a sleep and a forgetting;
The Soul that rises with us,
our life's Star,
hath had elsewhere its setting.
And cometh from afar.'

William Wordsworth

★ ★ ★

I suggest that if you can, leave the questions of the mind behind. As we know, the mind can never really be satisfied or comprehend anything beyond its quite limited capabilities.

Remain with your heart. Only the heart knows the Truth of you and what you really are and where you came from. All deep, profound realizations come from the heart.

★ ★ ★

Every human being who lives long enough will walk the path you are on. Take comfort knowing that you are not alone. Let your heart swell with compassion for this world and all its sentient beings, which will experience beginnings and endings and births and deaths as you have done.

Draw on the Love you feel for your beloved to empower your heart so that you can Love more and more. You are not meant to Love only one person. You are not meant to Love only the members of your own family or your friends. The immensity of your heart is for all. You have the capacity to Love everything and everyone in Creation as deeply as you Love and have loved your beloved. As Albert Einstein said,

'Only a life lived for others is a life worthwhile.'

Buddhist meditations on the practice of Loving Compassion often begin with instructing the meditator to first think of someone they cherish and Love very much. When the Love is summoned as a tangible force, the meditator is asked to send that very Love outwards to all sentient beings.

The practice of Loving Compassion does not make you Love your dear ones less. It helps you to Love them even more. Let the fulfillment of your heart be the inheritance of your Love. There is no greater gift you can receive from Creation or give to Creation. There is no greater meaning to your life, birth and death.

★ ★ ★

For the duration of your life allow times of sacred space to prepare for your own transition into The Great Mystery. You cannot know when your own or another's death will happen. Even when expected, it is always a surprise. In the meantime, cultivate friendship with the permanent and the eternal, with the devout and the Enlightened, so that you can easily recognise your True Friend when your time to journey further arrives. Be truly grateful that you have arrived this far.

★ ★ ★

'Hardly one among thousands realizes that life lives, and death dies.'

Inayat Khan

★ ★ ★

Dear One,

We have reached the end
of this special time
of respect and remembrance.

As I talk to you now,
are you already in a new womb
newly formed and excited,
waiting to be born?

Perhaps we will meet again
in bodies different from the ones we know
and we will Love and help one another
because our Love will flow,
regardless of deep recognition
or a vague,
distant, feeling of knowing.

I know now, my dearest one,
that all that matters is Love
Dear One,
I Love you
forever and ever

Amen

Nachiketa

This story is set in ancient times and has been handed down generations of thousands of years. It comes from the Katha Upanishad about the time approximately 1800 BC. The tale is of a remarkable young boy whose courageous meeting with Death Itself ultimately reveals the secrets of life and death.

During this time of Vedic history, the giving of donations was considered a great religious act. There were many ways to donate or sacrifice. Some gave everything they had. Others gave the best they had. One criteria however, was that the giver should not tell anyone what they have donated. This ensured that the donator's ego did not get too inflated.

At this time, there lived a well-known pillar of society named Uddalak. He was known for his generosity and knowledge. Uddalak had reached the peak of material and worldly success. There was nothing left for him to achieve but spiritual success. That is, sufficient grace to go to Heaven. He wanted to make sure that he would be well-taken care of in the Afterlife. One of the requirements to receive the grace he desired was that he give away his wealth to the learned and the poor. Uddalak was being asked to give up everything he had. All that made him powerful - especially his ego. After all, poor people are not respected - only rich and influential ones are honoured and made a fuss of.

He decided to hold a large function and make a grand public offering of all his cows to the local temple. Cows were legal tender in those days and they were worth a lot of money. Uddalak declared to all that he was giving away his possessions. People were very impressed. But Uddalak's son, Nachiketa, was aware that things were not as they seemed.

Firstly, he found all the pomp around his father's generosity, gross and pretentious. He was also aware that contrary to what his father was saying, he was not giving away all his wealth. In fact, he was handing over a herd of old cows on their last legs and was keeping the best ones for himself. Nachiketa was shocked. How did his father expect to cheat God?

Nachiketa was a very special boy. He was not only courageous but his honesty and clarity was like a laser beam that cut through his father's dishonesty right to the core. "Father, how can you say you are giving away all your possessions when all you are doing is handing over a bunch of old cows that are as good as dead?" he cried to Uddalak. "What makes you think you can cheat God like this? How can you think you will get a place in Heaven when all you are interested in, is how to impress your friends?" he continued ardently.

Nachiketa's father was furious. He was angry, embarrassed and humiliated to be so exposed by his son. How dare his Nachiketa be so disrespectful and scathing towards him? He held back his anger and said nothing. But Nachiketa had the bit between his teeth and he could not let it go. He went on. Finally, he asked the fatal question which made his father erupt and which changed everything forever.

"Are you going to give me away to the temple also, Father?" Nachiketa confronted him. "After all, I am your possession too, am I not?"

Nachiketa's father exploded. "No... I give you to Death!"

Uddalak did not really mean what he had said. And he regretted the words as soon as they were out of his mouth. They had come from anger. But they had been voiced and they could not be taken back. Nachiketa had made a valid point. It was the norm in those days for a young boy to be given to a Spiritual Master for instruction in religious studies and meditation. But, the way in which he had provoked his father made Uddalak lash out at him in anger.

Uddilaks words had a profound effect on his son. "How can my father even say these words to me," Nachiketa thought. " How can he wish to wipe my life away just like that because I have confronted him? How can Love change to anger and hate so quickly... and from my own father... Would he, could he, really mean to send me to Death?"

This momentous exchange between father and son revolutionized Nachiketa's life forever. A door opened inside his heart, which could never be shut again. It was an awakening. Nachiketa's entire world as he knew it crashed and the remains rushed through his heart like a vortex into the unknown. He had not thought about Death before, but now it was as though laid out before him to look at and really see what it meant. He realised the Truth. He saw something most people prefer to avoid. That millions had died before him and would continue to do so. He clearly saw how everyone and everything ends in Death.

His father's words, "I give you to Death" reverberated in his mind again and again. "What purpose is there to life if everything dies?" he wondered. "I will go to Death," he decided, "but not as others go, never to return. I will go voluntarily. I will meet Death and learn the meaning of life from him and I will return."

Nachiketa's Father was horrified. "What have I done," he despaired "And what will I do without my son. Who will look after me?" He felt frightened. Sadly, more for himself than for the boy.

"Look Nachiketa, I didn't mean what I said to you," he pleaded. "I said it out of frustration. You were annoying me. I just exploded?" he went on, hoping to change the boy's mind.

But, Nachiketa stood firm. The awakening had confronted him with questions of his existence. He wanted them answered. He viewed his father's words as a blessing. What was important to him now was to find the answers to the questions stirring in his heart. "Father, you told me I am to go to Death. You cannot go back on your words. You know one should never do that. To Death I am going!"

The way to Death is a long, deep inner journey. Nachiketa knew this and immersed himself in meditation, until he was barely breathing. This was an incredible feat of courage and single-mindedness for a boy so young. His mind and body became so still that he was as good as dead. Nachiketa crossed the frontier of his mind into the land of Death. He arrived. But Death was not there. He had gone out!

Nachiketa stood waiting at the gate. He had got this far and he was not going to budge. Death's wife and his attendants fussed around the boy telling him to go back from where he came. "Why do you want to stay here," they admonished him. "People want to run away from here, not come to visit," they told him ironically. "Look there's no point in waiting. No one comes looking for Death. Death goes in search of who he wants," they chided. "It's not the other way around." But Nachiketa stood firm. He was determined. This is the kind of determination anyone needs to get to the Truth

"I'll wait," he thought. 'For as long as it takes."

Nachiketa waited for three days and three nights without water or food. Death finally arrived and stood before him. He was immediately impressed by the boy's patience and his daring and courage. His sharp visionary eyes took in the innocence and the purity of the boy's heart. "Interesting," he thought, rubbing his dark chin. He knew it was not the boy's time to come and yet he had made such an effort to be there.

"My boy, I was not here to greet you. Please accept my apologies." Death regretfully told Nachiketa. And he meant every word. He already respected Nachiketa very much. "Let me give you three boons to atone for the three days and nights you have waited for me in this dark and hostile Realm."

Nachiketa was touched by Death's kindness. He had been told how cruel he was. That Death was a monster who placed a noose around his victim's necks and pulled them to his deathly abode. It was true that he was built like a mountain and he had eyes that bore through into one's soul. But this caring giant standing in front of him was not cruel at all. He was considerate, gentle and generous. And he had no rope!

"My Lord," Nachiketa asked, "My father is so angry with

me and he does not Love me as he once did. I am worried about his soul. Bless him please so that his heart is free from anger. Bless him, so that when I return to him he will be happy to see me."

Death was deeply touched by the young boy's unselfish request. Nachiketa cared more for his father's eternal life and soul than his own. He could have asked for anything, anything at all and Death would have given it to him without any conditions. "What kind of boy is this," Death wondered. He was happy to grant the boon. He promised "When you return, all will be well and your Father will welcome you with great Love and happiness just as he did on the day you were born."

"What is your second boon, my son," Death asked.

"I have heard that there is a state of consciousness one can reach that is vital and free of the ravages of age. I have been told that it is to do with the secret of a sacrificial fire. My Lord," Nachiketa pleaded, "Please tell me what this sacred fire is and how I can obtain it?"

Death could hardly believe that a boy so young would ask such a question. What Nachiketa was referring to was Prana - the fire of life - the fire of the Kundalini. Prana is life and when Prana is absent, no life exists. Death explained how the symbolic meaning of the sacred sacrifice is the offering of one's desires and passions to the Higher Will. Death told Nachiketa that when this happened, an immense Pranic energy becomes available in the form of Kundalini. Death continued to explain to Nachiketa, "When you live for the greater purpose rather than the lesser purpose, this fire is ignited deep within you and like a burning serpent, it rises through your being, purifying all in its way until the True you emerges glorious and radiant."

Nachiketa's heart was ignited on hearing Death's words. He dedicated himself to the task there and then. He knew that there was nothing more worth doing than this. And he had Death to guide him. What better time to go ahead, than when Death himself was with him to lead him step by step.

Death had no option but to instruct the boy. Nachiketa sacrificed all his desires, one by one, into the burning fire. The Kundalini fire ignited deep within him and arose. The serpent fulfilled its task. Only one desire remained within Nachiketa. The burning desire for Self-realization.

Death was now more than impressed. He was in awe of this courageous, pure, soul. "But, can he stay strong?" he wondered, "Will he fall back, like so many before him?" He thought. "Let us see..."

"Nachiketa, ask me for your third boon?" Death demanded imperiously.

"I ask for the secret of life and death," Nachiketa said as though he was asking for a piece of cake. "I want to know without any doubt if there is more than Death - if it is possible to go beyond Death. And if so, I want to achieve this."

"Nachiketa... Do you really know what you are asking?' Death gasped in amazement. "This is a very difficult thing to understand... Much as though I am impressed with your courage and determination, I don't know if you are really up to it. Even those in Heaven can't do it. The enticements to enter Maya are too strong."

But Death's answer only made Nachiketa all the more resolved.

"There is no other boon I want," the boy said with determination. "I want to go beyond death."

"Look," Death said to him, "Ask me for anything and I'll give it to you. Anything... anything at all. What most people dream of. Beautiful wives, luxury, sons and grandsons, the best life you could possibly have... Elephants, the wealth to feed the elephants... long, long life. Hundreds of years if you want it... "

"Why would I want anything that you will take away from me?" the boy interrupted Death. "Even if I had the world, one day, you would still come for me and take me away and I would lose everything. We both know that there are no pockets in a shroud," Nachiketa said resolutely.

Death was astounded. He could not tempt the boy with any of it. He could not deny Nachiketa's determination and truth. Death knew that he had no choice but to grant Nachiketa the incredible third boon.

And so, Death taught the young boy how to be the Master of his own energy - of the Pranic forces and channels that flowed within him. He instructed him, "All treasures are transient and I eat them up in the end. Attachments to the temporary world of names and forms lead to death. When you follow the senses, and you let them lead you, all you are doing is galloping along the road of sensory satisfaction. This road can give you nothing but exhaustion, depletion, frustration and death.

"What do you think you can do about this Nachiketa?"

Death asked his student.

"I can choose to change direction and go on another road," the boy said calmly and surely. He knew where the first road would lead him... Straight into Death's open mouth.

Death nodded his head. "Good." He responded, in continuing awe of Nachiketa.

"But what do I need to do on the other road?" Nachiketa had to know.

"Nothing", smiled Death. "Just don't go the first way."

"Stay still?" Nachiketa was getting it. "Don't even try to enter Heaven?" Now he was really getting it.

"Yes, but staying still takes effort. It requires a lot of vigilance and determination." Death continued, "But remember, it's only this way that you will find that you are not the body, nor the mind, nor the ego. It is only this way that you find you are The Self."

Death's words hit Nachiketa's mind like a bullet. There was an explosion of Light. He understood. The final stage transcends all the Heavens and all the worlds. It is untouched by them. It transcends the need to achieve anything or be anywhere. Death was telling him to let everything fall away and that what remains is pure Consciousness. Consciousness, he realised cannot die. It cannot be born and it cannot die. Death cannot touch it. The Eternal cannot be known by the impermanent. Nachiketa knew that when all desires and passions are removed, when perfect stillness prevails, the mortal becomes the immortal.

He realised that he and God were One - the One essence of Consciousness. It was so simple. The drop merged with the Ocean and Death could lay no claim on him ever again.

Nachiketa felt tremendous gratitude to Death. The great Master had enlightened him. Death felt the greatest bliss as he witnessed his student become the Master. They embraced. There was no need to say anything at all.

The boy, aware of his Oneness with God and his immortality, returned home. I like to think that on the way he sang this song:

'Wonderful am I!
In spite of the body
and its properties,
I am One.

I go nowhere;
I come from nowhere,
I abide in my Self,
pervading the whole Universe.

Praise be to me,
I am most skilful,
I, without a form,
uphold the Universe
through all eternity.'

The Ashtavakra Gita

* * *

What You Can Do

Mandala of Love

Paint a large circle. Surround it with images of the Divine and Divine Love. Within the circle, draw or write symbols of the time you had together with your beloved. Paste photographs of memories that you shared with one another. Use colour and natural objects in celebration and honour of your connection and Love.

Make an Affirmation

Make an affirmation in honour of who you have become and what you have learned because of having known your loved one.

For example:

I affirm that I, (your name) have increasing Love in my heart and in my life because of the grace of having known (your loved one's name). Because of our meeting, I can now more fully embrace life and Love.

Let your loved one live on in you in this wonderful way.

Make a Commitment to Remember and Honour.

There are times when we particularly remember our loved ones, such as the yearly anniversary of death or times in certain traditions where the dead are honoured. In the Western world, Christmas and New Year are family orientated and are often poignant times of remembrance for those no longer with us.

There is now a UK Day of the Dead, inspired by the importantly celebrated Mexican Day of the Dead, Dia de Muertos, which is held annually on one weekend in April. Each year has a different theme, with events which have included an art exhibition, death-related poetry, music and theatre, a coffin-making workshop, debate on euthanasia, discussion on Near-Death Experiences; and a co-ordinated open day at natural burial grounds.

Traditionally the Day of the Dead is celebrated on 31 October, the eve of All Saints' Day. However, The Natural Death Centre holds its Day of the Dead in springtime as a metaphor for hope and renewal.

The Chinese also hold a public holiday, Qing Ming Jie, for the annual family gathering at ancestral gravesides. Qing Ming Jie means 'Clear Bright Day', and is also known as 'Tomb Sweeping Day.' The Chinese believe that those who carry out all their family obligations will receive more fulfilment and happiness. The Ching Ming ritual is a great way to bring the family together. It is a family reunion, gathering at the cemetery every year.

When I was in Bali some years ago, I was invited by local friends to attend private functions in honour of the ancestors. I was also invited to an elaborate day festival in honour of the dead which is held annually. The participants dress in traditional attire and prepare sumptuous dishes of food in honour of all the ancestors. It is thought that if they are not honoured, no good can come to the family. The food is made with Love and offered to the dead to provide nourishment for the soul-bodies of the deceased. It is only after this offering that the people will eat and celebrate.

These rituals help us to commemorate our loved ones and remind us of our own mortality.

You may not be able to attend a large function like the ones above, but you can annualy remember, honour AND celebrate the memory of your deceased loved ones in a way that feels appropriate for you.

Remembering and honouring is not the same as having attachment. On the contrary it is about moving on, yet being grateful for what one has received through the blessing of your connection.

Let us celebrate the gifts we are given in our lives and be truly grateful for them. People are precious. Life is precious. The very personal and unique gift of loved ones with whom we share our lives, is very, very, precious.

Notes

19. *Sathya Sai Baba has revealed that his life is actually part of a Trinity of Sai Avatars. The first incarnation of the Sai Trinity was Shirdi Sai Baba (who embodied Shiva). The second incarnation of the Sai Trinity is Sathya Sai Baba (who embodies Shiva Shakti). The future incarnation of the Sai Trinity is Prema Sai Baba (who will embody Shakti).*

The incarnation of Shirdi Sai Baba (1838 to October 15, 1918) laid the base for secular integration and gave mankind the message of duty that is work.

The mission of the present Avatar, Sri Sathya Sai Baba, born November 23, 1926, is to help humanity realize that God or Divinity resides in everyone and that people should respect, love and help one another irrespective of caste, colour or creed.

It is believed that Prema Sai Baba will be born in a village near the city Mysore, India in the year 2021. This third manifestation of the Trinity shall promote the message that not only does God reside in everyone, but everyone himself/herself is God. Sai Baba has indicated that Prema Sai will herald the beginning of what is called The Golden Age, where Peace will prevail on Earth.

Coda

Dear friend, we end this sacred time together with the inspiring Divine words of Sai Baba. Let us enter the Pilgrimage of life in its fullness with a commitment to Love.

Thank you for sharing this sacred time with me. May we all be blessed to reach our fullest Divine potential.

'Life is a pilgrimage where man drags his feet
along the rough and thorny road.
With the Name of God on his lips,
he will have no thirst;
with the Form of God in his heart
he will feel no exhaustion.

The company of the holy will inspire him
to travel in hope and faith.
The assurance that God is within call,
that He is ever near,
will lend strength to his limbs
and courage to his eye.

Remember that with every step
you are nearing God;
and God too takes ten steps towards you
when you take one step towards Him.

There is no stopping place on this pilgrimage;
it is one continuous journey,
through day and night;
through valley and desert;
through tears and smiles;
through death and birth;
through tomb and womb.

When the road ends and the Goal is gained,
the pilgrim finds
that he has travelled only from himself to himself,
that the way was long and lonesome,
but the God that led him unto
it was all the while in him,
around him, with him and beside him!

He himself was always Divine.
His yearning to merge in God
was but the sea calling to the Ocean!'

Sri Sathya Sai Baba

Credits

1. *A Compendium of the Teachings of Sri Sathya Sai Baba, compiled by Charlene Leslie Chaden, Sai Towers Publishing, Bangalore, 2002.*

2. *Advice on Dying and Living a Better Life, by His Holiness Dalai Lama, translated and edited by Jeffrey Hopkins, Ph.D., Atria Books, NY, 2002.*

3. *The Ashtavakra Gita by Hari Prasad Shastri, Shanit Sadan, 1992.*

4. *Bardo of Becoming by Mynavati, Sai Towers Publishing, Bangalore, India, 2004.*

5. *Dalai Lama, My Son, by Diki Tsering, Penguin Books Ltd, England, 2000.*

6. *Death Must Die, The Diaries of Atmananda, by Ram Alexander, Indica Books, Varanasi, 2000.*

7. *Death - The Final Stage of Growth by Elisabeth Kubler-Ross, Prentice-Hall, Inc. USA, 1975.*

8. *Faith in God - A compilation of 250 Quotations on Faith in God from Sathya Sai Baba's Divine Discourses by Sri Sathya Sai Books & Publications Trust, Prashanti Nilayam, India.*

9. *Garuda Purana, compiled by B K Chaturvedi, Diamond Pocket Books (P) Ltd., New Delhi, 2000.*

10. *One-Liners - A Mini-Manual for a Spiritual Life by Ram Dass, Bell Tower, Random House, Inc., USA, 2002.*

11. *On Living and Dying, by J Krishnamurti,*
    Morning Light Press USA, 2005.

12. *Play of Consciousness, A Spiritual Autobiography by Swami*
    Muktananda, by Chitshakti Vilas, Chitshakti Publications,
    Chennai, 1994.

13. *Sathya Sai Speaks Series vol.1-XXVII – Discourses by*
    Bhagavan Sri Sathya Sai Baba, Sri Sathya Sai Books &
    Publications Trust, Prasanthi Nilayam, A.P., India.

14. *Snacks for the Soul, and More Snacks for the Soul, by*
    J. P. Vaswani, Sterling Publishers (P) Ltd., New Delhi, 2000.

15. *Tales and Parables of Sri Ramakrishna, Sri Ramakrishna*
    Math Printing Press, Chennai, 1943.

16. *The Bhagavad Gita.*

17. *The Book of Secrets by Deepak Chopra, Harmony Books New*
    York, New York, 2004.

18. *The Dalai Lama's Book of Wisdom by His Holiness the XIV*
    Dalai Lama, Thorsons, An Imprint of Harper Collins
    Publishers, London, 1999.

19. *The Geetha Vahini by Bhagawan Sri Sathya Sai Baba,*
    Sri Sathya Sai Books & Publications Trust, Prashanti
    Nilayam, India, 2005.

20. *The Gnostic Gospels, including The Gospel of Mary Magdalene*
    compiled and transcribed by Alan Jacobs, Sacred Texts,
    an imprint of Watkins Publishing, London, 2005.

21. *The Gospel of Peace according to Guru Granth Sahib, Duncan Greenlees World Gospel Series, The Theosophical Publishing House, Chennai, India, 2001.*

22. *The Holy Bible.*

23. *The Notebooks of Paul Brunton, vol.2, The Quest, Burdettt: Larson Publications, N.Y., 1986.*

24. *The Power of Now by Eckhart Tolle, Yogi Impressions Books Pvt. Ltd, Mumbai, India, 2004.*

25. *The Prophet by Kahil Gibran, Srishti Publishers and Distributors, New Delhi, India, 1998.*

26. *The Seven Spiritual Laws of Success by Deepak Chopra, Excel Books, New Delhi, 2000.*

27. *The Tibetan Book of the Dead, translated by Robert A F Thurman, Bantam Books, New York, USA, 1994.*

28. *The Tibetan Book of Living and Dying by Sogyal Rinpoche, Rider, UK, 1992.*

29. *The Upanishads.*

30. *Wake Up and Roar, Volume 2, Satsang with H W L Poonja, Pacific Center Publishing, Hawai, 1993.*

31. *The Wheel of Life by Elisabeth Kubler-Ross, Bantam Books, London, 1998.*

32. *What Becomes of the Soul After Death by Swami Sivananda, The Divine Life Society, Himalayas, India, 1992.*

Suggested Reading

1. *After Death: How People Around the World Map the Journey After Life* by Suki Miller, Touchstone, New York, 1997.

2. *Be Happy with Prayer, Meditation and Affirmation* by Mynavati, Cosmic Power Press, India 2002, email: Mynavati27@hotmail.com

3. *Chakra Power-How to Heal the Emotions*, by Mynavati, Sai Towers Publishing, Bangalore, India, 2004.

4. *Cutting The Ties That Bind* by Phyllis Krystal, Sai Towers Publishing, Bangalore, India, 2003.

5. *Divine Play* by Mynavati, Sai Towers Publishing, Bangalore, India, 2003.

6. *Facing Death and Finding Hope: A Guide to the Emotional and Spiritual Care of the Dying* by C. Longaker, New York, Doubleday, 1993.

7. *Glimpse After Glimpse: Daily Reflections on Living and Dying* by Sogyal Rinpoche, NewYork, Harper Collins, 1978.

8. *Heal* by Mynavati, Cosmic Power Press, Bangalore India, 2002, email: Mynavati27@hotmail.com

9. *Heaven and Hell* by Emmanuel Swedenborg, (1776/1923), Dent, London.

10. *Making Friends With Death: A Buddhist Guide to Encountering Mortality* Boston, Mass, Shambala Publications, 2001.

11. *The Natural Death Handbook, contact Michael Jarvis on 0871 288 2098*

12. *Other Lives, Other Selves by Roger, J. Woolger, HarperCollins, London, 2003.*

13. *Sleeping, Dreaming and Dying: An Exploration of Consciousness With the Dalai Lama, Boston, Mass by F Varela, Wisdom Publications, 1997.*

15. *Snacks for the Soul, and More Snacks for the Soul, by J. P. Vaswani, Sterling Publishers (P) Ltd., New Delhi, 2000.*

16. *The Celtic Book of Living and Dying by Juliette Wood, Duncan Baird Publishers Ltd., London, 2000.*

17. *The Soul Purpose by Dinah Vanswol-Jarvis, Sai Towers Publishing, Bangalore, India.*

18. *The Truth Is by Shri H.W.L. Poonja, Vidyasager Publications, San Anselmo, California, USA, 1995.*

19. *What Becomes of the Soul After Death by Swami Sivananda, The Divine Life Society. Himalayas, India, 1992.*

Information on The School of Ancient Wisdom can be found at the following website:
www.schoolofancientwisdom.org

Information on Bhagavan Sri Sathya Sai Baba and his Ashram and teachings can be found at the following website:
www.sathyasai.org